D0005376

The Instant Home Repair Handbook

by

Dick Demske

Illustrated by

Leonard Shortall

Published by

CAREER INSTITUTE

555 E. Lange Street   Mundelein, Illinois 60060

Instant Home Repair Handbook

A quick reference guide for the home handyman

Copyright © 1973 by
CAREER INSTITUTE, INC.
Library of Congress Catalog Card No. 72-91408
Printed in the United States of America

ISBN 0-911744-13-4

HR 73-2

Contents

Contents

Introduction

The INSTANT HOME REPAIR HANDBOOK is written to provide practical how-to-do-it information for the home owner who is interested in (a) the quick emergency repair, (b) a regular schedule of preventative maintenance, and (c) tackling a major home improvement project. The book covers all of the constantly recurring repairs required in a home—be it a major crack in a basement wall or a loose shingle on the roof. It provides handy checklists to allow the home owner to spot trouble in all areas before they grow into emergencies. Included, too, are instructions for improvements that add value to a home, such as paving a driveway or finishing a basement.

Step-by-step instructions and informative illustrations will aid the do-it-yourselfer in attaining professional results as well as in saving costly repair bills.

CHAPTER 1

Home Repair and Maintenance

A newly built home is a formidable work of man. In spite of the all-too-frequent shortcomings and failings of contractors, tradesmen, inspectors, and others involved in its construction, the average house is built to last at least a lifetime. Barring serious structural flaws, it can last several lifetimes—with proper care. The vital factors in keeping a home in good shape are regular, routine maintenance and periodic improvement.

1

Maintenance simply means the performance of such weekly, monthly, or annual tasks as mowing the lawn, draining the hot water heater, cleaning out the gutters, and checking for termite invasions. An improvement can be just about anything that adds to the value, appearance, comfort, or convenience of the house. In the broad sense, it can mean adding a room, a patio, or a whole new wing. It can mean putting a recreation room in the basement or turning the attic into another bedroom.

But improvement can also mean keeping your home abreast of the times by updating and upgrading. When it was built twenty years ago, for example, the home boasted a bright, attractive kitchen that was a delight to work in. How is it today? Unless it has been improved, not so bright or attractive. By updating it, you don't really have a "new" kitchen in the literal sense of the word, but you do have a modern, efficient, and—once again—bright and attractive one.

A combination of routine maintenance and periodic improvement will help to keep your home young—regardless of its age. True, over the years the costs may increase as a new heating plant, new wiring, new plumbing, a new roof, and the like are needed. But if you take good care of the home and keep decay under control, major renovation costs should be minimal.

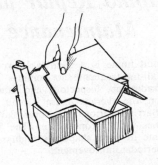

Do-It-Yourself or Call in the Professional?

Adhering to a routine of normal maintenance procedures should help you to avoid the kind of major breakdowns that necessitate emergency calls to the professional repairman—a burst hot water heater, for example. Almost all of these procedures can easily be done by the home handyman or his wife (and many can even be performed by the children, if you can get them away from the television set). The investment of a little money for maintenance and repair materials may also be required, but it's far cheaper than letting things go until you have to pay a high "rescue" price to a professional called in to bail you out.

There are some relatively major undertakings that may

or may not require the services of a professional, depending on your degree of skill (and initiative). Painting and wallpapering are examples. It does not take a great deal of skill or experience to paint a house or paper a room, but there are certain tricks and techniques that can save time and effort and assure more satisfactory results. If you know how to do these jobs—and can find the time and energy—you can save several hundred, or even thousands of dollars just by painting and papering your own home.

At the other end of the scale are major breakdowns, such as in the electrical system. If your house is more than twenty years old, there is a strong chance that the wiring is inadequate. With the many modern appliances in general use today, most such homes need extra circuits, 220-volt lines and the like. This is a job for the professional. In a very old home, the wiring may be positively dangerous, and should at least be inspected by a licensed electrician. (Of course, some older wiring is actually safer than that in newer homes because individual wires may be far apart or inside pipes, creating much less of a fire hazard. But again, only a competent electrician can judge this.)

Looking for Trouble

In most areas of life, it does not pay to look for trouble. Home maintenance, however, is one field where looking for trouble may bring you benefits rather than just more trouble. Some parts of a house are more prone to wear and deterioration than other parts, and you should know where they are. More important than knowing, you should inspect these sections regularly (in most cases, at least once a year) to try to detect problems before they become major. Then you can make the determination as to whether you can make repairs yourself or call in the professional.

Typical of these areas requiring periodic inspection are those listed below. Complete repair and maintenance details for each area are given in subsequent chapters.

• The roof. This should be inspected in the spring and fall, and after any severe storms, for bent or broken shingles, loose flashing, and the like. Roof problems that are ignored can become magnified many times, causing deterioration of sheathing and rafters and damage to ceilings and walls inside.

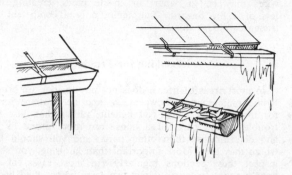

• Gutters and downspouts. If these are not properly carrying away roof water, damage may be caused to foundation plantings or gardens. In addition, wood may become rotted in areas where water is allowed to accumulate.

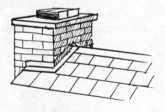

• Chimneys and flues. Stopped-up flues can cause heavy smoke damage; keep them clean. Chimneys *should* last as long as the house, but the mortar between bricks must be repointed occasionally. Check for cracks now and then as well, especially after severe storms.

• Television antenna. A properly installed antenna should withstand all but the most violent wind and storms. Give

6

it the once-over every year to make sure it's up there securely and that all supports are tightly fastened.

• Windows, doors, shutters. Small cracks and loose hinges should be repaired before they become big holes or fallen-off doors. Small sections of rotted wood should be scraped clean and patched. These chores should be part of a general spring or fall checkup; if you let them go, you will wind up replacing the whole door, shutter, or whatever.

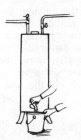

• Hot water heater. Properly cared for, this appliance will give you years of service. It should be drained monthly to draw off any rust that has accumulated, and inspected annually for any signs of tiny leaks that could become big ones.

7

• Plumbing drains. Periodic cleanouts are cheaper and easier than having to resort to an electric auger or calling a plumber after the drain is completely stopped.

• Septic tanks and cesspools. Do not mess (the word is used advisedly) with these, other than adding chemicals as recommended on a regular basis. Have an expert inspect them once a year.

• Electric appliances and motors. So many appliances are built-in today that they are often bought and sold as part of the house. So too, they should be a part of your regular home inspection. Check them out annually and replace worn parts. You can do this with the aid of your owner's manual. A serviceman may be called in to do the job, but this is the expensive way.

• Paint. You can let inside painting go for quite a while before serious damage may result (your rooms may *look* pretty bad, though). But outside, paint is vital to the preservation of the wood siding and trim (unless it is of redwood or red cedar). Check the exterior paint yearly and spot-prime any bare areas. Plan on painting the outside every three to five years (preferably in the fall).

• The attic. Sometimes a roof will seem perfectly sound from the outside, yet an inspection of the attic will disclose telltale dark splotches on the underside of the sheathing; perhaps it will even be wet after a recent rain. Try to determine where the leak originates (it may not be directly above the wet spot—water often runs along a rafter or other framing member before it becomes visible). If the leak is near a valley (where two roofs

8

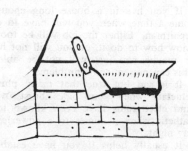

adjoin) or near a roof opening (such as for a chimney or a plumbing vent) strongly suspect the metal flashing. This can be patched with asphalt compound, but if it shows signs of irreparable old age, replace it.

If all efforts to find the source of a roof leak fail, you may have to tear off some of the shingles in the suspect area and inspect underneath. And if you still cannot pinpoint the problem, call in a professional roofer. Under no circumstances should you give up and let the problem go uncorrected.

• Basement or crawl space. Check for damp spots or cracks on concrete or masonry foundations and floors that may indicate leakage. Patch cracks so that water will not penetrate and freeze, causing further damage. Check all exposed framing—particularly that which is in contact with masonry or is close to the ground. Decay usually starts low, then spreads to the rest of the house.

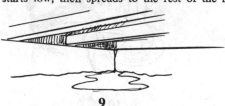

When You Have to Call a Professional . . .

If you live in a house long enough, there will surely come a time when you will have to call in a professional repairman. Either the job will be too big, or you will not know how to do it, or you will not have the proper tools, or maybe you just will not be able to spare the time. This can present some problems.

It is sad but true that many plumbers can be pretty reluctant when your pipes burst over a long weekend. And electricians have been known to be notably unsympathetic when it comes to a powerless house on a Saturday night.

It usually helps if you have established a certain rapport with the various tradesmen before emergencies arise, and if they recognize you as a "regular" customer. For example, have the furnace man check out and clean your furnace on a regular basis, even though you may not think it needs it. (It probably does.) When your remodeling plans call for a new bathroom, have the plumbing installed by a neighborhood tradesman, one who handles emergency calls as well as such installations, rather than by a "bathroom specialist" who will not be available when your basement is flooded. Doing it this way may cost a bit more on your bathroom project, but it will be well worth it if your cry for "Help!" when a pipe bursts on a frosty winter night is promptly answered.

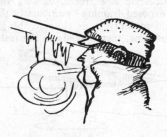

When you do have the plumber, furnace man, electrician, or whomever in to do a job, make it clear that you expect to be his customer from now on. A word of praise for work well done does not hurt either. Ask for his card and try to get his home phone number as well as his business, in case of emergency. While he is at your home, repeat your name several times so he does not forget it. Prompt payment of the bill also helps. It all sounds like a bit too much, but if it helps you to get service quickly when you need it, you will be rewarded for your efforts.

Your Professional Team

Assembling a list of competent tradesmen is itself a difficult task. There are good and bad ones, honest and dishonest ones, and there is no foolproof method of selection. You can lower the odds against you by talking the problem over with friends and neighbors, asking them about their experiences and whom they might recommend. They can also advise you about promptness of service and prices.

If you are new in the neighborhood and do not have anyone to consult, look in the yellow pages. *Before* you have trouble, call a few plumbers, a few electricians, a

few furnace men. Ask if they have emergency service, and how much they charge for a service call. While not as good as personal recommendations, at least this will give you some idea of what to expect when the need arises. It's a lot better than calling in a moment of desperation.

The Better Business Bureau maintains files on firms against which significant numbers of customer complaints have been registered. Check with them if you have any doubts about a firm with which you might deal. While not all such complaints are justified, discretion suggests avoiding the high scorers in this department. But do not expect the bureau to recommend a serviceman to you— that is not its function.

The Better Business Bureau and many consumer groups have for years been warning against door-to-door "furnace inspectors" and "home improvement" or "show house" salesmen. Still, these con artists flourish, so it may be helpful to repeat the warning once again. There are, of course, legitimate operators in these fields, which is what enables the crooks to keep going. Your best course is simply to refuse any door-to-door solicitations for home repairs or improvements, no matter how attractive or compelling the offers may seem.

What about Insurance?

The wise homeowner will take out insurance against most of the disasters, large or small, that can befall his home. This is as much a part of home care as routine maintenance. In fact, the holder of the mortgage will almost certainly insist on fire insurance as a minimum. In addition, a "homeowner's" policy will protect against several more perils (or at least pay for the damage resulting therefrom). Some bad loss experience on the part of the insurers is rendering the fine print in such policies a bit more stringent than it used to be, but the homeowner's is still a pretty good insurance buy.

12

Details of the policies differ from state to state and company to company, but generally their coverages are similar. Most run along the following lines, according to the common nomenclature:

HO-1 (Basic Form, or "A" in some states)

As does the standard fire policy, this policy covers damage from fire, lightning, removal from endangered premises, windstorm, and hail. In addition, it covers damage caused by

- explosion
- riot
- aircraft
- vehicles
- vandalism and malicious mischief
- theft
- smoke
- glass breakage

HO-2 (Broad Form, or "B" in some states)

In addition to the coverages afforded by the standard fire policy and the HO-1, the HO-2 covers damage caused by

- falling objects
- weight of ice, snow, and sleet
- collapse
- freezing of plumbing, heating, and air conditioning systems and appliances
- accidental discharge, leakage, or overflow of water or steam
- accidental tearing asunder, cracking, etc. of a steam or hot water system or appliance
- damage from certain electrical surges or accidents

*HO-5 (Comprehensive Form, or "C" in
some states)*

This policy has an entirely different concept than HO-1 or HO-2. It is a so-called "all-risk" policy, which means that it covers anything that happens to your home except for certain specific exclusions. In this instance, the burden of proof is shifted from you to the insurance company. They must show that any damage is caused by one of the *un*insured perils—otherwise you collect. In HO-1 and HO-2 policies, *you* must provide evidence that the damage was caused by one of the insured perils.

The perils that are *not* covered by an HO-5 policy include

- earthquake
- flood
- landslide
- war and nuclear radiation
- deterioration, wear and tear
- seepage from below the surface of the ground
- surface water
- smog
- vermin and insects

While far more comprehensive than other homeowner's policies, HO-5 is also considerably more expensive. Most homeowners settle for the lesser coverage.

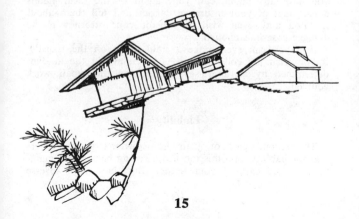

Making a Claim

The importance of regular home maintenance is pointed up by the list of perils covered and not covered. Notice that not even the most expensive policy covers "wear and tear," nor does it allow for damage caused by insects such as termites. If you have an HO-5 policy, you still cannot sit back with the notion that, no matter what happens, the insurance company pays. Get out and make those repairs before it is too late.

On the other hand, you should be well aware of just what your policy does cover. For example, it does not make much sense to go to the trouble of patching up your living room ceiling yourself if the damage is covered by "accidental discharge of water." Even if your careless child left the faucet on in the bathroom overhead and inundated the room below, the damage would be covered by such a policy. It would also be covered if the pipes broke—but the repair of the pipes themselves would not be covered, just the resultant damage.

If your house suffers any damage from water, electricity, wind, or anything else that you suspect might be covered by your insurance, check the policy closely. If you have any doubt, call your agent or the local claims department of your insurance carrier and tell them about it. You may even wish to consult your attorney if the damage is serious enough.

And you can even make a mild profit on the tragedy, if you wish, by collecting on your claim (in the amount determined by an appraiser) and doing the repair work yourself.

Liability

The second part of your homeowner's policy covers you for liability, and this too has a strong bearing on maintenance and care of your home. But there is a reverse

twist here—the insurance company covers your negligence if you *do not* maintain your property. (Of course, the insurer will defend you even if you are not negligent.)

By terms of such a policy, the insurance company will defend you against lawsuits brought against you because of alleged negligence. This could mean many things— failure to supervise your children, to keep your dog on a leash, or to keep your steps in safe condition. If the mailman trips over a hole in your sidewalk, or a neighbor's child gets clobbered by a falling gutter, you are protected up to $25,000 by most standard policies. In a sense then, the insurance company is your last line of defense in terms of home maintenance. If you do nothing at all to keep your property in shape and someone gets hurt as a result, at least you have that much protection.

But it is far better to fix that hole in the sidewalk, the corroding gutters, and the loose steps *before* somebody gets hurt. If you do all these things, you are still covered by your insurance, of course. But you have a much better chance of winning any lawsuits that arise and protecting yourself against any damage awards in excess of your insurance coverage. In addition, you will enjoy peace of mind.

17

Is It All Worth While?

When you buy a home, you are inevitably buying work. You cannot simply let things go until little problems become big ones—not unless you are willing to pay the big costs that go with such neglect. Unlike a car, you cannot run your house into the ground, then junk it and buy another.

But there are more positive aspects to regular home maintenance. For example, when you want to sell your house, you can certainly ask a better price if everything is in order. At any other time you can avoid showing the shabbier parts of your house, but for potential buyers you will have to bare all. Then, if you have kept up the homestead all through the years, you can be proud and confident to show it off to people. The good care will be evident, and you are likely to get your asking price.

But that is in the future. There is a good "now" reason for keeping your home in top shape. That is simply that it feels good to live in such a home. A well-cared-for home is one you can learn to love and be proud of. And the neighbor's grass will never, ever look greener.

CHAPTER 2

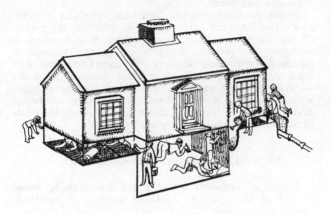

Foundations, Basements, Crawl Spaces

A home very literally rests on its foundation, and can be no better than what is beneath it. Any imperfections or problems in this area should be promptly attended; anything that could lead to the weakening of the structure must be corrected immediately, or extensive damage may result.

Fortunately, serious foundation problems are rare. Poured concrete walls set on properly placed footings should exhibit no major problems unless extensive settling occurs and is neglected for a long period. A concrete block wall may show the effects of poor workmanship, resulting in a loose mortar bond. But this should be noticed long before the damage is severe enough to cause any real trouble.

By far the most common basement complaint is dampness. The basement may contain as much as 50 percent of the usable space in a house—space that is wasted if it cannot be utilized, if only for storage, because of dampness or periodic flooding. A damp basement may cause problems of dampness in other areas of the house as well. And the dampness may be a warning of more serious troubles. Such a condition should never be ignored, but before corrective action can be taken, the cause of the dampness must be pinpointed.

Leakage, Seepage, or Condensation?

Almost all basement moisture problems can be traced to one of three causes: leakage, seepage, or condensation.

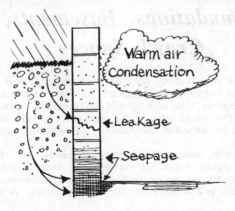

Leakage usually occurs during a heavy rainfall, or when snow is melting away. An excessive amount of water is built up in the soil around the foundation walls, forcing its way through any cracks or other defects in the walls. If the area around the walls has been improperly backfilled or graded, the situation is aggravated. In very wet periods, considerable flooding may result.

Seepage is evidenced by large areas of dampness on the basement walls, rather than water leaking through a crack or other defect. Usually, the dampness will be greatest along the bottom of the wall, or at the wall-floor joint. Like leakage, it is caused by excessive water pressure on the outside of the basement walls. It may also be due to capillary action, which actually draws water from the moist soil through porous spots in the masonry.

Condensation looks very much like seepage, but in this case the moisture is coming not from outside the walls but from the air inside. It usually happens in warm, humid weather, when the cool masonry walls seem to "sweat." But it can also occur during colder months when warm air is discharged by a clothes dryer or similar appliance; moisture from this air collects on the cooler walls in the form of tiny droplets, which may be mistaken for seepage from outside.

A simple test will determine whether a damp wall is the result of seepage or whether condensation is the cause. Tape a small mirror to the wall (or use a waterproof mastic if it is too wet for tape to stick). Leave it there overnight and inspect it the next day. If the surface of the mirror is fogged, the moisture came from inside the basement, and condensation is the villain. If the face of the mirror is clear and dry while the surrounding wall is still damp, blame it on seepage.

Patching Holes and Cracks

If leakage is the problem, your first step is to plug the leak. This is best done with a quick-setting hydraulic cement, available at any hardware store. This cement can be used even when water is coming through a crack or other defect (such as the area around the wire ties used to hold foundation forms together during construction). If the crack is dry, you can mix your own concrete patch with 1 part cement to 2½ parts sand.

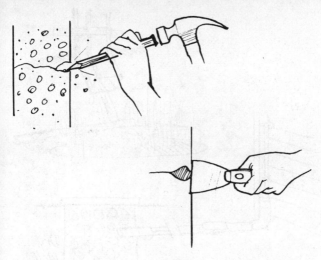

Before patching, use a hammer and cold chisel to widen and undercut the crack (½ inch at the surface, wider beneath so that the patch will be locked in place). Clean out all loose rubble, then thoroughly dampen the area. Force the patching mixture into the crack with a trowel. Allow it to dry thoroughly, then apply a waterproofing compound to the repaired area.

Diverting Surface Water

Patching holes and cracks solves the immediate problem of leakage but, since the ultimate cause is excess water accumulation in the ground around the foundation walls, this situation should also be corrected. Seepage, also the result of such accumulation, is similarly corrected by making provisions to carry off water before it can come in contact with the foundation.

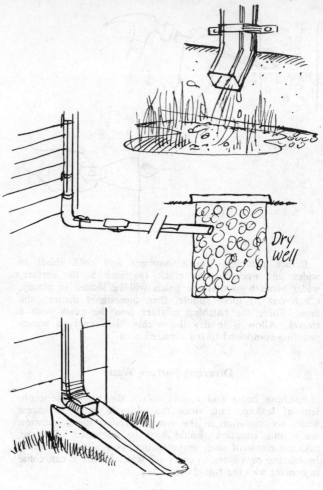

First, check gutters and downspouts for leaks or improper pitching that allow water to collect along the foundation wall. Gutters that are clogged with leaves and other debris may also divert water onto the ground alongside the house. Downspouts should be connected to a storm sewer (or, in some localities, the sanitary sewer), or to an underground dry well located at least 10 feet away from the foundation. Downspouts that are not so connected should empty onto a concrete splash block that diverts the water away from the walls.

In order to carry away rainwater as quickly as possible, soil should slope away sharply at foundation walls, then more gradually to at least 10 feet from the walls. If such is not the case, fill in with new soil, taking special care in areas where puddles form during rainy weather. Sow the graded area with good grass seed or sod and roll it down evenly and firmly. If the new grading extends above basement windows, protect them with a curved metal shell or a concrete wall. Gravel in the bottoms of these protected areas will facilitate drainage, and hinged covers may be provided to close them up when it rains or snows.

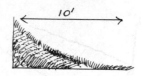

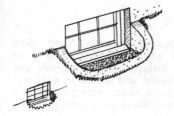

Where concrete walks or driveways are adjacent to the foundation wall, they should also slope gradually away. The walk-wall joint should be rounded or sharply angled to keep out water. If joints are not so protected, or if they are broken or otherwise damaged, they should be corrected.

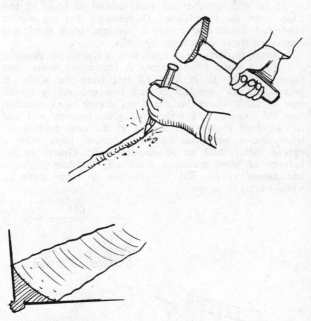

Chip away loose or damaged concrete. Scrub clean both the wall and the walk where new concrete is to be bonded, and roughen both surfaces with a hammer and cold chisel. Moisten the surfaces, and trowel in a mortar of 1 part cement to 2½ parts sand, sloping it sharply away from the foundation wall for 2 to 3 inches.

Underground Drainage

If your home is in a very low, wet location or is built over a marshy area or an underground stream, it may be necessary to install a system of drain tiles to carry away excess water. Excavate alongside the outside of the foundation wall to a point beneath the level of the basement floor (but not beneath the footing that supports the foundation). Lay drain tiles of clay or plastic in the trench, sloping them gently to discharge lines that are led to a storm sewer, dry well, or similar outlet. Cover the joints between the tiles with strips of tarpaper to prevent sediment from penetrating the tile line. Then surround the tiles with crushed stone or gravel 18 inches to 2 feet deep and replace and regrade the soil on top.

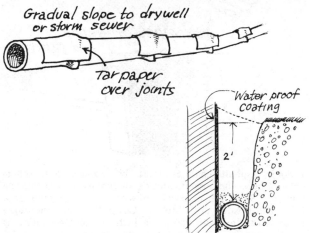

Gradual slope to drywell or storm sewer

Tarpaper over joints

Water proof coating

2′

If you have gone to the trouble to dig a trench along the foundation walls to install drain tiles, you might as well be thorough and waterproof the outside of the walls as well. This, along with your other efforts, should cure just about any problems of leakage and seepage.

First scrub the concrete clean to remove all dirt and sand. An asphalt coating is recommended. Apply a priming coat of the material thinned with kerosene to the consistency of paint. Use a large brush, and apply liberally. The thin mixture will soak into the pores of the concrete, providing a good bond for the next coat.

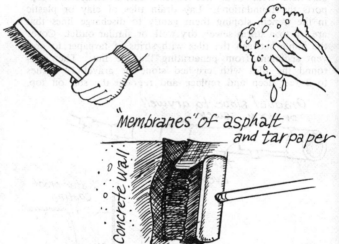

"Membranes" of asphalt and tarpaper

Some asphalt coatings must be applied hot, others cold. Check the manufacturer's directions before starting the job. Swab the material on with a roofing mop or a fairly stiff-bristled push broom. Cover the walls thoroughly to a thickness of about ⅛ inch. A single coating is usually sufficient, but for added protection, you can build up "membranes" of alternate layers of asphalt and heavy tarpaper. The number of layers used depends on the moisture conditions to be overcome.

After the final coating, carefully backfill to avoid damaging the membrane. Regrade, sloping the soil away from the foundation.

If your problem does not require the installation of drain tiles but is serious enough to consider waterproofing the exterior of the foundation, consult a professional. Equipment and materials are available to force waterproofing compound through the soil under high pressure, with little or no excavating required. This is not a do-it-yourself job, however. And be forewarned: While there are many highly reputable firms in this basement waterproofing business, there are also many of lesser reputation. Follow the usual practice of checking with the local Better Business Bureau and other homeowners who have dealt with the firm before you sign any contract. As ever, buyer beware.

Treatment of Interior Walls

Although attempting to stop leakage or seepage by applying some type of material to the inside of basement walls is generally ineffective, it may work where seepage is minimal.

If used in conjunction with previously described methods, the coating of interior walls will provide additional protection against dampness.

A layer of mortar (1 part cement to 3 parts fine sand, mixed with just enough water to make a thick paste) can

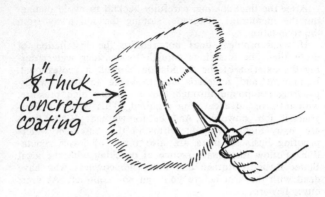

⅛" thick concrete coating →

be applied. This should be troweled on to a thickness of
⅛ inch. Also available at most hardware stores is a special "waterproof" powdered cement that is mixed with water
and brushed onto the basement walls. Whether using mortar or powdered cement, the walls must be clean and
porous, and preferably unpainted. If the walls have previously been painted with oil or latex paint that seals the
surface, the old paint must first be removed. A chemical
remover will do the job. If the walls are whitewashed,
scrub them with a dilute mixture of muriatic acid (8 to
10 parts water to 1 part acid). Wear rubber gloves for this
job, and be careful not to splash any of the mixture on
your skin. If you do, wash it off immediately with plenty
of water.

Before applying mortar or powdered cement, wire-brush
the walls, then dampen them thoroughly. Two coats are
recommended, especially along the lower parts of the
walls. Overlap the floor to help seal the wall-floor joint.

Several types of waterproof paints are available, but
these are more decorative than protective. Follow manufacturer's directions carefully when using these. Some
types require special primers.

30

A two-part epoxy resin compound is very effective as a sealer against hydrostatic pressure, but it is expensive and somewhat difficult to apply, so it is generally used only along the wall-floor joint where leakage problems may occur. The material is mixed immediately before use and brushed or troweled into place. Two coats are usually required.

Condensation Cures

If your mirror on the wall has become fogged, indicating that your basement dampness problems are caused by condensation, the remedy is to dry out the air in your basement as much as possible.

Adequate ventilation is essential for a dry basement. In cool, dry weather, keep the basement windows open. On damp, hot days, keep them closed; warm, moist air may result in mildew or condensation upon the cooler masonry walls. If your basement has too few windows to provide needed ventilation, an exhaust fan can be installed.

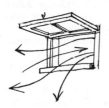

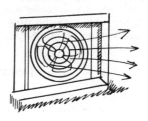

Where condensation persists, an electric dehumidifier or chemical drying agents may be needed to remove the moisture from the air.

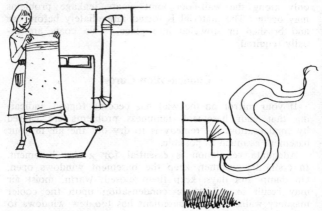

Clothes dryers should always be vented to the outside. This is a relatively easy do-it-yourself job. Use a sabre saw or keyhole saw to cut a hole through the wall (usually between joists) after first drilling a pilot hole. Insert a hooded fitting through the hole from the outside, then connect the dryer's exhaust port to this fitting with flexible pipe. Both the fitting and pipe can be purchased at most hardware stores.

Finally, try to avoid hanging clothes to dry in the basement. The moisture from the clothes will become condensation on the walls.

Concrete Floors

Minor floor cracks are repaired in the same way as cracks in foundation walls—by undercutting and patching.

But where major damage or widespread seepage is a problem, a new concrete topping must be installed.

First clean off the old surface, then apply an asphalt coating or membrane layers as described for wall treatment. Pour a layer of concrete approximately 1 inch thick over the old floor, then place a reinforcement of lightweight steel wire mesh and pour another inch of concrete, troweling it smooth. Keep the concrete moist for several days to prevent its drying too rapidly. (Slow drying is necessary for the concrete to reach its full strength.)

Dusting is a more common problem with basement floors. The surface becomes powdery and somewhat messy. Fortunately, the cure is not too difficult. Brush the floor, then wash it down thoroughly with water. When dry, apply wax or a coat of concrete paint.

Crawl Spaces

Crawl spaces present some special problems because cold and dampness commonly invade these areas. Occasionally, unpleasant odors result. These conditions make living on the floor above somewhat less than ideal. But the conditions are usually curable.

Again, adequate ventilation is essential. There should be vents or louvers on at least two opposite sides of the crawl space to provide cross-ventilation. If necessary, you can install vents by cutting holes through the walls between joists, or by knocking out a concrete block if your foundation is of that type. Louvered vents, which can be closed off in damp or cold weather, are best. Most of them are also screened to keep out rodents and other small animals. You can buy these vents at any building supply house.

Cold floors over crawl spaces present another problem. The best solution is to install 4-inch insulation batts to the floor joists. Staple the batts to the bottoms of the

33

joists, forming an air space between the subfloor and the insulation. Below the insulation, staple a vapor barrier of heavy (50- to 90-pound) felt paper. This will seal out any moisture. Make sure that the entire area beneath the floor is covered.

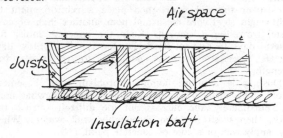

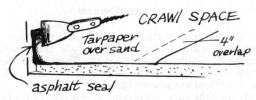

If dampness persists, cover the ground in the crawl space with tarpaper. Overlap the joints 3 to 4 inches, and seal the tarpaper to the foundation walls with asphalt compound. Then spread a 2-inch-thick layer of dry sand over the tarpaper. This should insure that the area above will be cozy, dry, and warm the year-round.

Termites and Dry Rot

While termites and dry rot do not directly affect the foundation of a home, they are generally first observed in the basement or crawl space. Both problems can be quite serious and, when they become noticeable, demand drastic and immediate attention.

A basic cause of both conditions is excessive moisture. Particularly susceptible are homes near rotted lumber—perhaps stumps or construction scraps that are buried next to the foundation because of careless backfilling. Wooden steps or fences in direct contact with the ground are also invitations to termites, whose staple food is wood.

In addition, if any of the conditions of dampness described previously are allowed to go unchecked, the danger of termites or dry rot is greatly increased. Unfortunately, this type of problem is often discovered too late. Termites eat wood from within and, except for kings and queens of their colonies, never surface, so that damage may go unnoticed until a structural member is practically hollowed out. But this process takes some time—perhaps years—and homeowners vigilance is a good defense.

If you suspect problems of this nature, inspect all wood under the first floor of your home. Probe any suspicious areas with an ice pick or a sharp knife. If the probe penetrates easily for more than about an inch under hand pressure, the wood has probably deteriorated.

To reach wood not in direct contact with the ground, termites build mud tubes or tunnels from the ground up along the foundation walls to the house sills. Whenever these are found, they should be broken open. Then check the adjacent wood areas for damage.

During mating season, the kings and queens leave the colonies to establish new ones. These winged insects are often confused with flying ants, but a close inspection will show that the termites are thicker waisted and have opaque, whitish wings, while the ant's wings are transparent. When they settle down in their new communities, the termites shed their wings. If you find a pile of such tiny wings near your foundation, this is another sure sign of trouble.

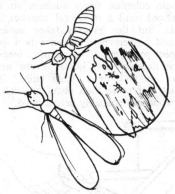

Termites thrive on wood, but they cannot live in it and must return to the soil at least once a day. Therefore, your most effective defense against them is to poison the soil around your house so that they cannot penetrate it. There are several preparations for this; most effective are those containing chlordane or heptachlor. Whichever you use, carefully follow manufacturer's directions for mixing and diluting with water. A trench 2 to 3 feet deep must be

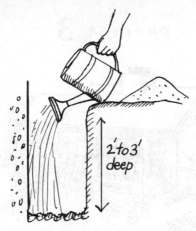

2' to 3' deep

excavated around the entire foundation. Part of the poison is poured into the bottom of the trench, and the remainder is mixed with the soil as it is replaced. This will provide protection for up to five years, and any termites remaining inside the house will quickly die off as they are prevented from returning to their colonies.

Dry rot is caused by a microscopic fungus growth. It is a harmless airborne organism until it finds damp wood. Then it multiplies and grows rapidly, feeding on the cellulose of the moist lumber. Dry rot is almost impossible to detect until it is in the advanced stages. Then the wood will have a spongy, cheeselike consistency when probed with ice pick or knife.

Wood that has been damaged by termites or dry rot must be replaced, after the conditions that have caused the damage are corrected. If the wood that has been damaged is an integral part of the house structure (joists or sills, for example), a professional contractor may have to be employed. You may want to use specially treated lumber to avoid similar problems in the future.

CHAPTER 3

The Outside
Wall

The outer walls of your home are your first line of defense against the elements. Cracks in masonry, loose or broken shingles, broken mortar joints in brick and brick veneer, clapboard that has split or sprung—all these will, if left unattended, weaken before the ravages of wind, rain, snow, and freezing temperatures and lead to major—and costly—deterioration outside as well as within.

Many of these conditions seem minor, almost innocent, at first blush and therefore go largely ignored by the busy homeowner, who seems always to have some more pressing matter to attend to around the house. But the effects are subtle, and do not generally show up until long after the time when a simple repair job would have done the trick. By then, of course, it is too late: unchecked condensation or leakage has damaged the walls.

A slow, thorough inspection for cracks and open joints should be made of all outside surfaces (it is wise to make

an annual program of this). Check particularly around windows and doors, and wherever two dissimilar materials meet—wood and masonry, for example, which expand and contract according to temperature and humidity. Hoist yourself up on a ladder and look for possible leak points at roof flashing, and around gutters and downspouts (discussed in Chapter 5). Be suspicious of outside walls enclosing laundry room, kitchen, and bathroom—minor damage here may indicate a condensation problem rather than leakage.

Caulking Windows and Doors

Used properly, the cartridge-type caulking gun is the homeowner's best friend. Available in any hardware store, paint-supply house, or lumberyard, the cartridge unit is an inexpensive item that contains sufficient compound for most crack-filling operations around the outside of the house. And it is much neater than the standard bulk-supplied caulking gun, as the cartridge can be disposed of after use. For small repair jobs, toothpaste-size tubes of the compound are available.

Unlike putty, caulking compound does not harden and become brittle; rather, upon exposure to air it forms a tough surface "skin" while inside it remains soft and flexible. Thus, it is a natural for use in filling cracks and open joints around windows and doors, and will last for many years before deteriorating—*if* it is applied correctly.

Check for cracks around all window and door frames and door sills, not ignoring even hairline cracks. Since the compound will not adhere properly to dirty or greasy surfaces, it is useful to invest a little time in preparing the affected area. Use a wire brush to clean out loose dirt and debris, then give the area a quick wash with any household detergent. Keep in mind, however, that the surface must be perfectly dry before the compound can be applied.

A common error made by many do-it-yourselfers is to apply new compound over old. Use a scraping tool or the blade of a screwdriver to scrape out the old material, if such exists, then prepare as above. If the area to be filled is wide, it may be necessary first to apply some filler material such as oakum, available in plumbing supply houses and some hardware stores. Fill to about 1 inch from the surface before caulking.

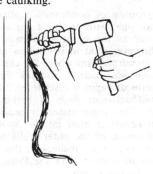

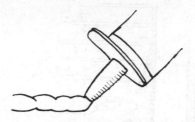

A little practice on the unexposed portions of doors or windows will enable you to apply a smooth, uniform bead of the substance. Use a smooth, even pressure on the trigger and aim for a convex bead rather than a concave one, since this is more efficient. If the repair work is being undertaken in cold weather, when the compound hardens and becomes difficult to manage, store the cartridge in a warm spot a few hours before use.

When appearance is not a consideration, the caulking compound can also be used to fill cracks in masonry.

Condensation Checks

The problem of condensation often is considered strictly an indoor one, with peeling paint and wallpaper and bulging plaster as the obvious indicators. Few people understand, however, that in bathrooms and kitchens and in insulated laundry rooms where the clothes dryer is not vented to the outside—indeed, around the entire house—water in the form of vapor is discharged into the air from normal household activities such as bathing, cooking, and dishwashing. This vapor naturally seeks the drier outside air and can penetrate most interior wall coverings, passing to the cold inside of the outer walls where it is returned to its liquid state. Left unchecked, this form of water leakage may saturate timbers and sheathing, ultimately forcing its way out through siding.

To protect against this, most newer homes are equipped with a continuous vapor barrier of some sort—usually batt-type insulation, which has tarpaper on one side, or stapled foil or plastic sheeting—between the inside and outside walls. If some repair or renovation work has upset the integrity of this barrier, the damaged section should be repaired.

In the absence of such a barrier, there is little one can do except to eliminate or reduce the problem at its source. This does *not* mean that you have to throw out the dishwasher or stop bathing: simply provide an escape route for the water vapor and prevent its accumulation.

It is as easy as opening a window after you bathe or while the kitchen is in use. A more satisfactory arrangement is to install exhaust fans in kitchen and bath and, in either case, form the habit of opening a few windows around the house a crack every day to provide cross-ventilation, which can be done without discomfort even in the chilliest of weather. In the laundry room, make sure the dryer's exhaust is vented outdoors (see Chapter 2)—this, and the exhaust fans mentioned above, comprise weekend projects within the reach of the homeowner handy with tools.

A simple test for excessive interior humidity is to look for signs of heavy condensation on the inside of windows. If the windows have storm sashes, open the windows and observe whether condensation forms on the inside of the storm sash. Keep in mind, too, that the attic must also receive adequate ventilation to avoid this sort of problem. Unfinished attics should be equipped with louvers that are kept open.

Repairing Wood Siding

Wood siding of either the drop or bevel type is generally applied over wood or composition sheathing and tar or building paper. If you live in a gentler clime, the siding may be nailed directly to the wall studs for economy purposes. Normally, a paint job every three to five years or so is all the maintenance it needs, but when faults show up they should be attended to at once. Warped or loose boards, open joints and blistered or peeling paint may signal leakage or condensation problems, and in themselves will contribute to the problem.

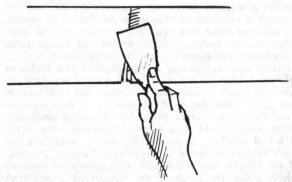

Simple, small cracks can be disposed of by filling them with caulking compound or lead-base putty applied with a putty knife. If the board has begun to work loose, drive in a couple of aluminum nails along the edges. When working with old siding which is subject to splitting, drill a pilot hole for the nail almost the same size in diameter. Such holes can be countersunk and the nail head covered with filler. Wait at least 24 hours before repainting over puttied areas.

Clean splits along the grain of a board can be corrected with glue. First gently pry up the loose portion of the split and apply waterproof glue along the split itself. Press the board back into place; then drive long finishing nails into the bottom of the board at an upward angle so that the split edges are pressed together tightly. Allow time to dry, then plug nail holes.

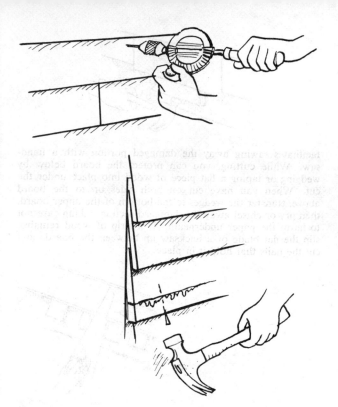

Warped boards can often be corrected by nailing; any gaps at the board ends are then filled with putty. Always drill pilot holes for the nails first.

Replacing a damaged section of board—or an entire board, for that matter—is not as impossible a chore as you might imagine. First drive wedges under the affected section so as to separate it *slightly* from its neighbor below; this

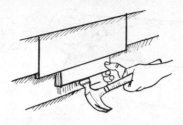

facilitates sawing away the damaged portion with a hand-saw. While cutting, you can protect the board below by wedging or taping a flat piece of wood into place under the cut. When you have cut on both sides up to the board above, transfer the wedges to the bottom of the upper board, then pry or chisel away the damaged section, taking care not to harm the paper underneath. If a strip of wood remains, slip the flat blade of a hacksaw up between the boards and cut the nails that hold it in place.

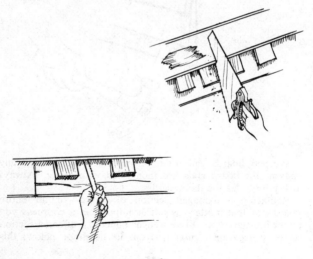

Use the old section of board as a template for the new piece, which is inserted into place by tapping it with a hammer from underneath. Use a block of wood to protect the new section, driving it until it lines up with its mates. Drive nails approximately 1 inch up from the bottom edge, then a second row of nails the same distance along the upper, overlapping, board. Before the new section is installed, you should check that the paper underneath has not been damaged; if it has been, apply a coat of roofing compound or asphalt cement to seal any openings.

Replacing Broken Shingles

Wood-shingled homes should be inspected regularly for broken, loose, or missing shingles or shakes. The repair or replacement procedures are fairly quick and simple in each case, and should be undertaken as soon as the defect is detected so as to avoid deterioration of surrounding shingles.

Sagging or loose shingles are usually the result of loosened nails, and sometimes hammering these back is enough to secure the shingle. If this does not work, an extra nail can be driven in 2 inches or so from the old ones; use serrated, rust-proof nails and exercise care not to damage the shingles while hammering.

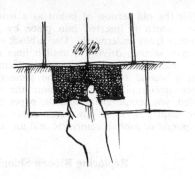

In cases where the shingle is cleanly split, you can make an effective repair by sliding a piece of waterproof paper under the shingle, then nailing the two sides tight at the split.

Since shingles overlap each other, replacing a broken shingle requires that you sever the nails securing it at the top. This can be done by slipping a hacksaw blade under the upper shingle and cutting the nail heads. Where shingles are nailed top and bottom, with a horizontal wood strip at the bottom to create a "shadow" effect, it is also

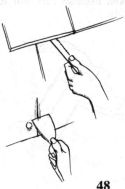

possible to chisel the wood slightly around the nail heads of the upper shingle and extract the nails with a pliers. It is then a simple matter to pry out the damaged shingle. Insert the new unit and nail the top and bottom securely. If a number of shingles have to be replaced in a single area, presoak them several hours before use to avoid having them pop loose during the first rain. They should be tightly butted at the sides when installed.

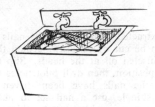

Asbestos Cement Shingles

These shingles are formed of Portland cement and asbestos fiber under high pressure. While generally maintenance-free, they are brittle and therefore require special handling during replacement.

First remove the old shingle by breaking it off piece by piece; a hammer can help here, but take care that your blows are neither too strong nor wide of the mark. The

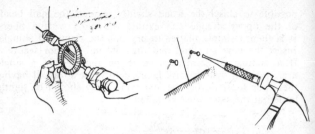

exposed nails can be extracted with pliers. The nails of the overlapping shingle can be cut by hacksaw, drilled through from the outside, or chiseled off at the heads. Slip the replacement shingle into position, then drill pilot holes for the securing nails. When the nails have been driven in to within ¼ inch of the shingle, use a nail set to put them flush with the surface: a hammer blow to the shingle itself will crack the material.

Cracks in asbestos board paneling should be corrected by replacing the entire panel, following the precautions for shingles.

Removing stains from this type of material can sometimes be a problem. Rusting metal on the house exterior—gutters, fastenings, window and door screens, electrical conduit—is the usual culprit. Rust stains on the asbestos-cement surface require use of an acid cleaning agent, then

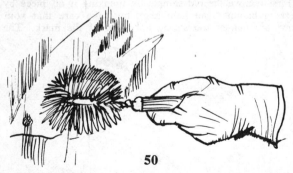

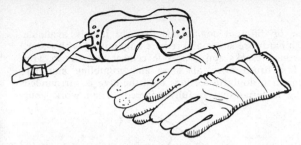

a rinse with clear, cold water. Ask your hardware dealer to recommend acid solution and strength, and remember to exercise extreme caution in use. Soot can be washed clean with a heavy-duty detergent.

Masonry: Patching Cement, Brick, Stucco

Masonry walls are made of either stone, brick or brick veneer, concrete block—bare, stuccoed, or painted—or stucco over wood or, more commonly, over metal lathing. In all cases, the homeowner must inspect for leak points —cracks, broken or porous mortar joints, and other surface faults—and correct these as soon as possible. Openings around windows and doors can simply be caulked (see section on Caulking), while repairs to other surfaces involve

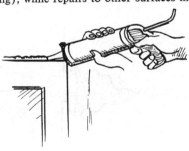

the use of different compounds that are largely available through hardware stores and require only mixing with water.

To repair cracks and gouges in cement and stucco, you must first brush away all loose and crumbling material, cold-chiseling doubtful sections until the area is surrounded only by material that is fully adhered. Then work your

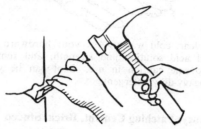

chisel so that the edges around the fault are wider at the bottom than at the surface: this will permit the patching compound to maintain a sure grip when dry. Wet the area to be patched thoroughly before applying the compound, then trowel it onto the desired surface finish.

When filling deeper cracks, it is desirable to make two applications of the patching material, the first to ¼ inch or so below the surface; allow 24 hours between applications.

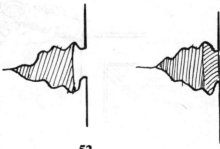

Since these compounds tend to "run" if carelessly mixed, you should follow the manufacturer's directions to the letter; generally, the mixture should contain enough water so that it holds its shape but will not crumble under troweling. Making two applications on the deeper repairs avoids this problem.

When filling wall corners that have been chipped or gouged away, the job can be made much simpler with the use of two-by-fours. Prop a section of wood in place so that it covers the gouge and lines up with the corner of the wall. Pack in the patching cement from the other side and trowel it flush with the wall. Then move the wood to that side and smooth the other surface, leaving the wood in place until the patch is dry.

Covering large patches of stucco demands a bit more effort. It may be necessary to rip out the damaged area to the lathing, or below it if lath is also damaged. If this is the case, proceed carefully until you have exposed the siding. Clean out the area to the good material, then install new tar or building paper with rustproof nails. Cut a section of 1-inch wire mesh or metal lathing the size of the patch and nail securely into place.

The stucco should be applied in three coats, with adequate time between applications. The first coat is applied with a wood trowel only to cover the mesh, working upward at all times. This coat should be "scratched," or "given tooth," while still damp, using the edge of a scrap of mesh or any serrated tool. Allow it to dry for 24 hours, spraying occasionally with a fine mist to keep it moist.

The second coat is applied smoothly to within ⅛ inch of the finished surface; a straightedge or metal bar should be used to achieve a level application. This coat must be applied onto a wet surface, should be allowed to harden for at least seven days, and itself be fully wet before the third coat is put on.

To apply the final coat (which may be mixed to a specific color), trowel it to a smooth finish that is flush with the old material, then work it to achieve the desired texture. Splattering on a thin mixture with a whisk broom will give it a rough texture. Waiting for the final coat to set slightly, then rubbing in a circular motion with a wooden trowel, will provide a smooth surface. You can experiment with other materials to obtain the texture you want.

Repair to brickwork and cement block is largely a matter of renewing defects in mortar joints. The work requires only a prepared mortar mix, hammer, narrow cold chisel, pointed trowel, and wire brush. Remove cracked or crum-

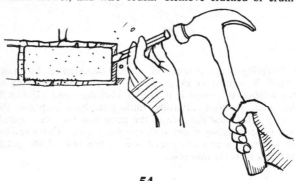

bling mortar with the chisel, then clean the cavity and wet it completely before applying the mortar compound. Use the point of the trowel to finish the job so that it matches the other joints; a concave joint can be made by pressing a pipe or dowel into the slightly stiffened mortar and trimming the excess.

It sometimes happens that the joints of an entire wall become porous due to age, or sloppy work originally, or both. If this is suspected, the least expensive solution is to coat the joints around each brick with a clear waterproofing compound—a time-consuming task, but less awesome than complete remortaring.

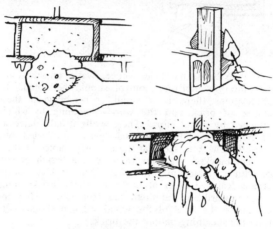

To replace a badly cracked or loose brick, carefully chisel out the mortar on all four sides, being careful not to disturb its mates, then remove the brick. Clean out the cavity, then wet it and coat the sides and back generously with mortar, meanwhile soaking the replacement brick in water. Coat the brick with mortar, press into place, and finish off the joints.

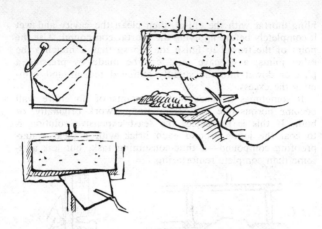

If your house has brick veneer walls, an additional consideration in moisture control should be noted. In such applications there is a small space between the single course of brick and the wood sheathing to which it is attached by metal clips. These walls usually have a series of holes along the base that permit collected water to run off. Check to see that these "weep" holes, if they exist, are not blocked, and free them with a length of stiff wire or with a ½-inch masonry drill. The drill can be used to create drainage holes at the base of the bricks: angle the holes upward and set them 1½ feet apart. They must be cut above the level of the wood sill and should not penetrate the sheathing behind the brick.

Cleaning Outside Walls

Cleaning the outside walls of your house of soot, grime, and stains is more a matter of maintenance than mere tidiness. Dirt buildup on painted wall surfaces can deceive the onlooker into thinking a new paint job is called for (a good paint should last at least five years), and stains not only are unsightly, but some types can lead to deterioration of the surface itself.

Walls can be washed easily with detergent and any of the siphon-type sprayers available in hardware stores, or by using a hose brush attached to a stick. Wash one side of the house at a time, working from the top down to prevent streaking. A strong industrial detergent and hand scrubbing may be necessary where the buildup of grime is severe.

A common stain that attacks new masonry is the whitish powdery deposit called efflorescence. It is caused by formation of salts in masonry that has not fully dried or is because of leakage. It is particularly unsightly when it attacks brick surfaces. This stain can be removed with a solution of 1 part muriatic acid to as much as 10, or as little as 4, parts of water, depending on the severity of the stain.

Work on small areas at a time, using a coarse brush or steel wool. Keep the solution from contact with skin and eyes—wear protective clothing—and prevent it as much as possible from coming into contact with other materials. When working with brick, for example, clean each brick individually and do not let the acid attack the grout or mortar. Wash the entire area thoroughly with clean water in liberal amounts after the cleaning operation.

A weaker mixture of the acid—1 part acid to 20 of water—will remove tenacious mortar stains from brick.

Soot stains on concrete can´ be lightened considerably, if not removed altogether, with a solution of ½ pound trisodium phosphate to 1 gallon water. Apply the mixture liberally to the affected area, permitting it to soak in, then scrub vigorously with a brush. Sometimes soaking a piece of cloth in the solution and adding abrasive powder will give better results than a brush.

Trisodium phosphate can also be used to remove mildew stains from wood surfaces. Mix a weak solution, about 1 ounce to a gallon of water, and add 8 ounces of household bleach. Give the mixture time to penetrate the wood, then fully rinse off.

To remove the greenish oxide stains from masonry, first scrub the area well with ordinary cleaning powder. Then prepare a solution of 1 part sal ammoniac to 1 part household ammonia. Soak the stain with this and rinse thoroughly.

CHAPTER 4

Walks and Driveways

Come springtime, the condition of the walks and driveway around your home should command your close scrutiny. It is a good time to inspect for and perform needed repairs on surfaces that show signs of winter damage, hint at costly future deterioration, or may possibly present a safety hazard (even more costly!).

With a little know-how and at small expense (relative to hiring outside contractors) you can perform these needed repairs yourself. It requires only a basic knowledge of

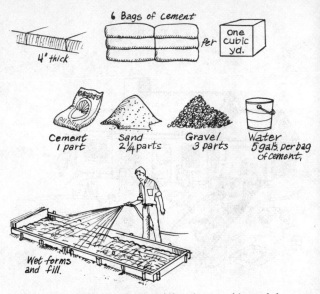

6 Bags of Cement per one cubic yd.

4" thick

Cement 1 part   Sand 2¼ parts   Gravel 3 parts   Water 5 gals. per bag of cement.

Wet forms and fill.

masonry handling and materials plus an idea of how to prevent major damage from occurring.

Whether the surface is concrete or blacktop, leakage is the major threat. Water by itself, finding entry through cracks or porous and pitted surfaces, will undermine the fill material and result in sinking or breaking up of top matter. When this water is frozen repeatedly in the course of a winter, it can result in frost heaving, a process not entirely unlike that which takes place with floes of ice.

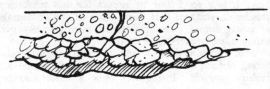

Thus cracks should be tended to at once, while they are still simple to repair. Grass and weeds growing through concrete are a sign that at least part of the walk needs resurfacing. Pits, loose rock, and even small collections

of water in blacktop indicate the possibility of trouble underneath, requiring either application of a waterproof sealer or spot patching or both.

Repairing Cracked Concrete

For small concrete repairs, the packaged cement mix available in hardware stores is your best bet. It requires only the addition of water to form a stiff, yet plastic consistency and it is easy to work with. Do not, however, simply stuff the material into the crack and consider the job done.

First use a cold chisel to open the crack cleanly along its length, widening it if need be to a minimum of 1 to 2 inches, depending on its original size. Make sure that all loose material is cleaned out, then either wet the insides thoroughly or apply any of the bonding agents sold for this purpose. Pack the patching mix into the crack with a trowel, working it in tightly to avoid shrinking as it dries. Wait until the compound has become watery before at-

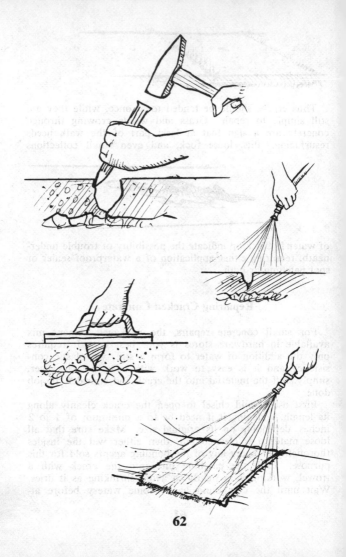

That ... the trade is enhanced while the soil ... still ample, to repair cracks and ... working through ... concrete ... a sign that ... drainage of the whole work must be ... resumed. For ... floors, leaks, and even small collections

of water ... to indicate the possibility of trouble under‑ neath, ... the application of a waterproof sealer or

Repairing Cracked Concrete

For small concrete repairs, the ... is usually available in hardware stores ... ... adding a ribbon of water to form ... ... when ... so it is easy to work ... scraping of the material into the crack ... ... done.
... rivet ... cold chisel to open the crack cleanly along ... its length ... and widen it a minimum of 1 to 2 inches deep ... and ... Make sure that all loose material ... ... Either wet the fresh ... ... mortar sets ... or ... sealer sets for this purpose ... ... the crack with a trowel, working ... pushing as it dries. When this ... concrete, where ... before air

tempting final troweling—use a wood trowel for a rough surface—and lay a piece of wet burlap over the repair to keep it moist for at least 72 hours.

When a piece of walk has cracked so that one side is higher or lower than the other, it is still possible to avoid total resurfacing. Lift the offending piece with a lever and fulcrum—a two by four and crowbar, for example—then prop it while you pack in or remove crushed gravel accordingly. Work this until the sections of the cracked piece are level, then finish as above.

When large sections of walk sink or are pushed up by unruly tree roots, the break usually takes place along the joints, or expansion lines in the concrete. A whole section can be levered up at both ends to correct a sinking problem—one end at a time, of course—and fill added to bring the section to level or the desired slope. The method here is to open the soil around the sides of the slab until you

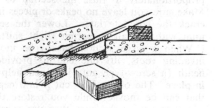

are below the concrete. Chisel the crack at the joint, if necessary to free the slab.

First pry around the sides to make sure the section is loose, then lever up either end to a height that will permit working a rake underneath. Do not try to lever it up all at once; do it in successive stages, chocking it at each step until you can slip a steady support under the end.

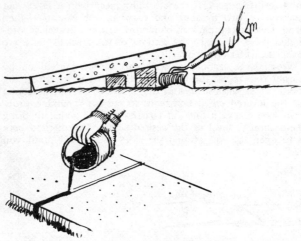

When working in the fill—either gravel or cinders—follow the contours of the underside of the slab, adding proportionately to raise the section to the height desired. Make sure you leave no peaks or pieces in the fill that would crack the concrete later. Lower the section, then fill the joint with asphalt to permit slight shifts without cracking.

When a large section has to be moved to clear away invading roots, lift one end to provide clearance underneath (a screw-type auto jack can help here) and prop it in place. The object is to cut it into neat, man-sized pieces that can be moved while you restore the ground. Decide where you want the cuts, then use a broad chisel to score in light, then successively heavier, cuts until the slab breaks

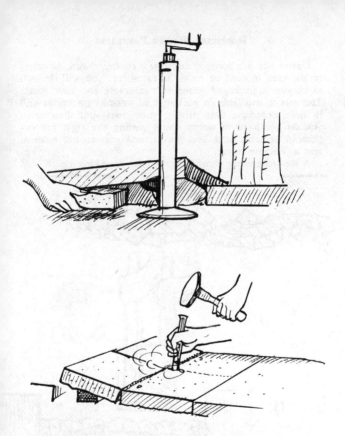

cleanly. The best place to start such cuts is across the center of the section, then down its length if four pieces are wanted. When the roots are removed and fill is in place, put back the pieces and cement the cracks between them.

Replacing Broken Pavement

Unless you are going to lay a new concrete walk or drive, or the area in need of repair is extensive, you will do well to choose a packaged gravel-mix concrete for your work. The mix is available in packages of various quantities and is more expensive than mixing your own—but then again you do not have to worry about getting the right proportions of cement, sand, and gravel, and you do not have to rent a concrete mixer.

A sledgehammer should be used for breaking up the old

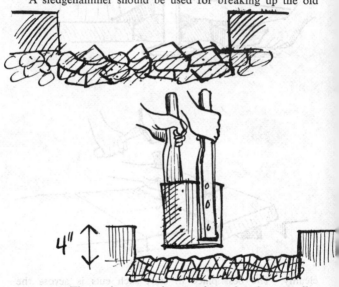

concrete. These pieces can in turn be reduced to smaller pieces for use as a base for the new mixture. The new concrete should be poured to a depth of 4 inches for walks and 6 inches for drives.

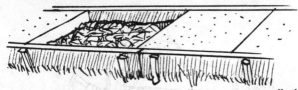

Chisel the edges of the surrounding concrete until the sides are straight or have a slight inward slope at the bottom edges. You will need a concrete form to support the material while it dries. This can be simply lengths of two-by-four or two-by-six lumber set on edge and supported by stakes along the sides of the patch. The top edge of the form should line up exactly with the surfaces of concrete on both sides of the patch.

Prepare the foundation for the new cement by raking in an even topping of crushed gravel, broken cement, or cinders. Tamp it down firmly—a heavy section of wood with two upright, lighter pieces nailed to its ends for grips makes an excellent, if primitive, tamper.

Even if you are going to use only a portion of the package of prepared mix, empty the entire bag and work the contents with spade or rake to assure an even mix of the ingredients; then return the unused portion to the bag before adding water. Do not add too much water, as this will weaken the strength of the patch; mix thoroughly to a stiff consistency.

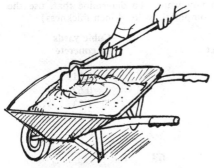

Shovel the cement into the form and level it off with a strike board which rests on the wood form (or forms, if a complete cross section of walk is being filled) and the old concrete. Use the board in a sawing motion across the new cement until it is level. Wait until the material stiffens slightly, then trowel and keep damp for several days—a week is even better.

When working with large areas, the premix concrete may not be practical. If the job is big enough, it may pay you to have ready-mixed concrete brought in a truck; this can be poured quickly and easily from a chute. Look in the yellow pages under "Concrete—Ready Mixed" for a supplier and tell him how much you want. To determine that, use the following table (all computations for 4-inch thickness):

Square feet	Cubic yards of concrete
10	0.12
25	0.31
50	0.62
100	1.23
200	2.47
300	3.70

For a 6'x20' walk, for example, multiply the dimensions to get 120 square feet. Add 1.23 for 100 feet, and .31 for 25 feet, for a sum of 1.54. If you have measured and dug correctly, 1½ yards *might* be enough. Play it safe, however, and order the next highest amount the supplier will sell you (probably 2 cubic yards).

As long as you are ordering, make sure you get the right concrete for the job. Here are some of the specifications to give your supplier:

1. Specify the amount of cubic yards, remembering to make allowances for uneven grades, spillage, etc. It is far better to have a little left over than to run short.
2. Specify at least six sacks of cement per cubic yard to insure a good bond.
3. Ask for not more than a 4-inch slump to insure the proper type of mix. A 4-inch slump, which is a measurement of consistency, will give you a good, workable mix. Stiffer mixes are harder to finish by hand. Mixes that are wet and soupy will not produce durable concrete.
4. Specify a coarse gravel aggregate with a maximum size between ¾ and 1½ inches. A 1-inch maximum is the ideal.
5. Ask for 6 percent (plus or minus one) "air entrainment" to obtain good durability, particularly in colder climates. Air-entraining reduces damage by frost and salt because it develops minute, well-distributed air bubbles in the concrete.
6. Specify where and when to deliver the concrete, and if possible place your order at least one day ahead of time.

If the job is inaccessible to concrete trucks, or too small to order in quantity, yet too big to use premix, you will want to mix your own concrete. For very small jobs, hand-mixing in a mortar box or somewhere else will not be too

69

difficult. For larger jobs, rent a portable mixer which can be used at the site.

The recommended mix for most home applications is 1 part portland cement, 2¼ parts sand, and 3 parts gravel or stone aggregate. Five gallons of water should be used for each bag of cement. For one 94-pound bag of cement, use 215 pounds of sand and 285 pounds of aggregate, plus the aforementioned 5 gallons of water. This should make a workable substance with a slump of no more than 3 inches. In northern climates, use air-entrained cement or add an air-entraining substance to the mixture.

Whether you mix your own or order it ready-mixed, do not be too independent. For best results, it takes at least two persons to place and finish concrete. For larger jobs, three people are recommended.

Placing Concrete

In preparing for the concrete, wet the ground and forms with a garden hose. Have a wheelbarrow handy for both ready and homemade mix.

Place the concrete in the forms to the full depth, spading along the sides to ensure complete filling. Strike off the concrete with a length of two-by-four board in a sawlike motion across the slab to smooth the surface of the concrete while cutting it off to proper elevation. Go over the

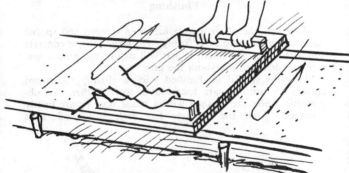

concrete twice in this manner to take out any bumps that remain after the first pass. This "screeding" process will make finishing easier. Any low spots should be filled before the second pass to provide a uniform surface for the finishing operations.

Immediately after striking off, work a big wood float back and forth across the slab to smooth it and remove irregu-

larities. Do not overwork concrete; overworking will result in a less durable surface. For areas around curves or in cramped spaces, use the small wood hand float to accomplish this smoothing operation.

Finishing

Make sure that the concrete has been tamped and spaded just enough to compact it firmly. On large jobs, a concrete compactor can be rented, which will assure the proper surface and density throughout the mix.

Sidewalks should be finished with a slightly roughened surface to insure a safe foothold in wet weather. To obtain this, walks are finished with a wood float or are lightly broomed. After the concrete has been struck off, it is

smoothed with a wood float or "darby," leveling any raised spots and filling depressions. Side edges are then rounded with an edger to prevent the concrete from chipping. Where necessary, the marks left by the edges of the wood float may be removed by brushing with a calcimine brush dipped in water.

In some localities, the smooth finish obtained with a steel trowel is still preferred. When steel troweling is done, it should be after all water sheen has disappeared and the concrete is so hard that no mortar accumulates on the trowel. This requires considerable effort on the part of the finisher to produce a satisfactory finish. Drawing the trowel over the surface of the concrete should produce a ringing sound. Excessive troweling is to be avoided as it tends to bring too much water and fine material to the top, forming a chalky surface.

Joints are placed in concrete sidewalks to take care of expansion and contraction caused by changes in temperature. There are two kinds of joints—expansion joints and contraction joints. (If you use air-entrained Portland cement, these problems are minimized.)

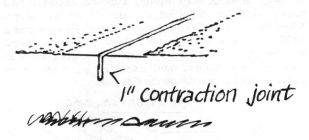

1" contraction joint

Contraction joints are simply separation planes between slabs. When the concrete shrinks in cold weather, these joints open slightly, thus preventing irregular and unsightly cracks. They are generally spaced at 5- or 6-foot intervals.

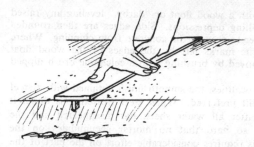

Contraction joints may be formed by cutting a slot in the slab about 1 inch deep. This forms a plane of weakness and, when the slab contracts, it will crack at this joint. The slot is cut by a T-bar forced into the fresh concrete to a depth of 1 inch. After the concrete has partly hardened, the bar is withdrawn and the joint edged with a double edger held against a straightedge to make a clean, straight joint.

Expansion joints consist of premolded material, usually ½-inch thick and as wide as the depth of the walk. They should be placed wherever the walk meets another walk, driveway, building, curb, lighting standard, or other rigid object. They are placed on all sides of the intersection. When the sidewalk fills the space between the curb and a building or wall, an expansion joint should be placed between the sidewalk and the curb and between the sidewalk and the building or wall. Expansion joints are not required at regular intervals in the sidewalk.

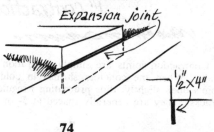

Expansion joint

½"x4"

Concrete must be cured so that it will be strong and have a durable surface. Curing can be done by keeping the concrete continuously wet for at least three days in warm weather and seven days in cool weather. This can be accomplished in a number of ways.

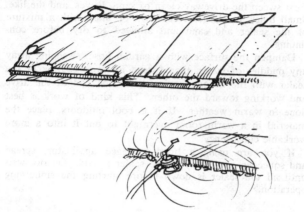

When the concrete is hard, moisten with a hose and cover with a plastic sheet weighted down around the edges. This will prevent rapid evaporation of the moisture. You can also cure by keeping the slab wet with a sprinkler or by covering with burlap or similar material and keeping the burlap moist by occasionally spraying with water.

Protection of Blacktop

To protect asphalt surfaces from weather, pitting, and porosity, and as a cure for minor cracks and shallow depressions, you can apply a coating of any of the coal-tar pitch or neoprene sealers available commercially. They are applied directly from the can (a 5-gallon can will cover approximately 200 square feet), require no special mixing or preparation of the surface, and are simple to work with.

The sealer can be applied with an old pushbroom. A special applicator, consisting of a broom at one end and a squeegee for finishing at the other, is available at low cost. First sweep the driveway clean of sand, leaves, and the like. Small holes and larger cracks can be filled with a mixture of the sealer and sand and allowed to dry before continuing.

Dampen the surface with a garden hose, sweeping away any puddles of water, then spread an even coating of the sealer with the broom, beginning at one end of the drive and working toward the other. This kind of work is best done in warm weather. If it is cool outdoors, place the material in a warm room overnight to put it into a more workable consistency.

If you are using a brush-squeegee applicator, spread and squeegee alternately as the sealer is laid. Do not wait until all the sealer is down before starting the smoothing operation.

Filling Holes in Asphalt

When sections of a blacktop drive have begun to crumble at the surface and sides, showing loose rocks, deep fissures, or consistent presence of water, it is necessary to dig up the damaged portion and lay in a patch of new asphalt. The work is quick and easy to perform and should be tackled before wear and weather contribute further to the erosion problem.

For this type of repair, the best material is a cold-mix asphalt compound which is premixed with fine gravel. It requires no heating as such; but if the weather is cool, store it in a warm room before use (its staining power is great, so protect your floor by placing some paper beneath the bag).

Break away the disintegrated asphalt with hammer, chisel, or shovel, until you are down to a firm base. To save on the patching material, place a few large chunks of rock in the bottom of the hole, then fill around these with gravel or cinder. Tamp this material until it is packed tightly.

Now add your patching compound directly from the bag to within 1 inch of the surrounding surface. Tamp this vigorously until it is compacted tightly, and all air pockets have been removed.

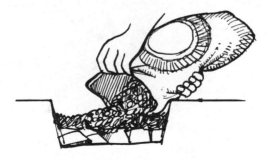

Fill the remainder of the hole with asphalt, adding until it is about ¼ inch above the surrounding surface. The final tamping operation can be begun by hand, but should be finished by driving your car repeatedly over the area. You can rub some fine sand on the patch beforehand to avoid picking up the fresh asphalt on your tires.

CHAPTER 5

The Roof

Because it is up so high, the average homeowner may avoid thinking about the condition of his roof until the need for repair becomes distressingly evident. And when that happens, he concludes that the only sensible thing to do is to call in the roofing contractor.

In truth, there is a good deal of plain common sense in such a conclusion. Reroofing your house (a garage or shed may be another matter) should be done by the expert. Severe damage and decay require skilled hands and quality materials to correct. It is just too important a part of the house to treat in an offhanded fashion.

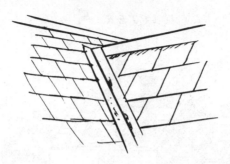

It is because of its importance that you should keep a constant watch on the condition of your roof. Leakage can cause serious damage to the interior of the house. Inspection and care of gutters and downspouts will avoid troubles with the walls and foundation.

While they are still minor, these checks and repairs can be handled by you at small expense in labor and dollars.

If you must call in a contractor for major work, invite several to bid on the job. Avoid the gypsy and deal only with a reputable specialist. If at all possible, hold the assignment until the time of season when he is least busy; it will be less expensive.

Getting Off the Ground

Don't wait until a leak occurs: stop it before it happens. A regular inspection of your roof's condition will turn up potential trouble points.

Look for loose, broken, missing shingling or slate. Old or poor quality wood shingles will often warp and cause leaks. Lightweight asphalt shingles can be twisted up at the ends as a result of high winds, particularly when the pitch

of the roof is steep. On roll-paper roofing, look for open seams or cracks in the material. Check for heavily corroded or loosened flashing under the eaves, around the chimney, and along the valleys formed where different angles of roof meet.

In unfinished attics and crawl spaces, finding the source of a leak presents no great problem. A careful inspection on a rainy day will show where the trickle begins. To spot it on the roof, drive a long finishing nail up through the leak point so that it protrudes on the roof (do not try this with slate).

If you wish to make a temporary repair until you can get to the job, coat the underside of the damaged area with roofing cement. Cut a piece of board to fit exactly across the rafters on either side of the area and toenail it in place, driving a single nail through each end at an angle into the adjoining rafter.

Damp and discolored ceiling plaster in finished attics is a sign of leakage, but only indicates the general area in which the leak may have originated. Keep in mind that water can be diverted from its point of entry, following rafter, sheathing and joist to affect plaster at some remote point.

You can make a rough measurement from the nearest outside wall to the discoloration and estimate where the corresponding point on the roof would fall. Once up on the roof, use this as a starting point and make a close inspection of the roofing material, working upward until a likely defect is discovered.

Ladders and Scaffolding

Despite the apparent ease and simplicity some roofers demonstrate in scampering about rooftops, no real professional goes up without taking adequate safety precautions. This should go double for the amateur.

Do not attempt any work on a rainy day: plug the leak from the inside or hang on until conditions are less slippery. To help give your feet purchase, wear rubber-soled shoes (sneakers are a good choice, but solid work shoes are better if you have to work up there a long time, as they provide better foot support).

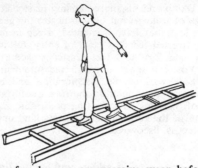

Test your ladders for damage or excessive wear before climbing them. You can place a wood ladder flat on the ground and walk on it from top to bottom—you will know if it will hold you. Make sure the ratchet mechanisms on extension ladders do not stick or give only partial hold.

To raise a ladder without strain, set its foot against the base of a wall, then lift the opposite end over your head and walk it, rung by rung, until it is upright. The correct position for the ladder's foot is one-quarter the length of the

84

ladder from the wall. The footing must be secure, of course. Extra stability can be obtained by driving a finishing nail partially into the edge of the roof alongside the ladder top. This offers some protection against side slip.

It is safest to use both hands when climbing. This is not always possible, as it will be necessary to transport cans of roofing cement or other materials. When doing this, make sure you have a place to set down your materials when you get to the top. If the angle of pitch is too great, a helper should be there to relieve you of the burden. Tools must be secure on your person, but within free and easy access. A carpenter's apron with its capacious double pockets is handy for storing roofing nails and cutting knife. A final word of caution: It is better to make lots of safe little trips up and down than to overburden yourself dangerously with tools and materials. And no matter how slight the incline you are working on, if a nail rolls from your grasp —let it go.

Some form of scaffolding is necessary if your roof is steeply pitched. There are several ways to construct such scaffolding. You can easily provide a safe footing by adding a support hook to the end of an extra ladder, which can then rest securely in place alongside your work area. This is done by nailing two strong pieces of wood to the end of the ladder. The pieces must be braced by shorter lengths of wood and angled so that they can be hooked evenly over the peak of the roof. Another way to do this is with a

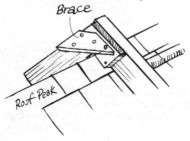

Brace

Roof Peak

long length of strong rope, tied at one end to the ladder and at the other to a tree or nearby support.

Take special care when walking on slate, tile, and asbestos shingle surfaces. These materials are brittle in nature and can be damaged by a clumsy foot.

Shingle Repairs

Asphalt shingles that have curled up at the ends can be repaired easily by applying a dab of roofing cement under each end and pressing down. If this condition is evident on a large area, begin at the bottom courses and work your way up. Small holes and simple cracks in these shingles can likewise be corrected with roofing cement. Nail down both sides of the tear with flat-head roofing nails, then paint the tear with the cement, making certain the nail holes are filled.

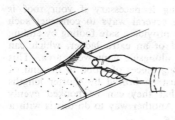

When entire shingles are missing or damaged beyond repair, extract any broken remnants then either remove or drive flat the nails that held them in place. A nail ripper

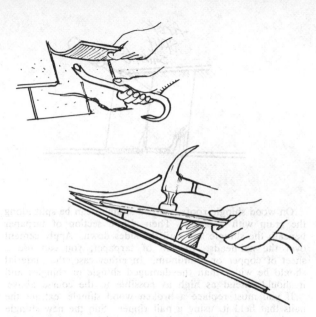

is a good tool for this; or you can carefully lift up the edge of the good shingle above, lay a flat bar of metal or a screwdriver over the nail heads and hammer them down flat. Insert the new shingle and nail it into place under the overlapping shingle above it. Don't leave nails exposed.

To replace the shingles along the ridge of a roof, first remove any fragments of shingle, then cover the exposed ridge with roofing cement. Ridge shingles are cut from whole shingle, which normally produces three pieces. If you are replacing more than one, nail the lower corners of each piece to the top of the shingle beneath. The pieces should overlap each other by 2 inches. When you get to the last shingle, slip it under the shingle above and nail its top corners so that the nailheads are covered.

On wood shingle roofs, warped shingles can be split along the grain with a chisel. Then slip a section of tarpaper beneath the shingle and nail the sides down. Apply cement over the nailheads. Instead of tarpaper, you can use a sheet of copper or aluminum. In either case, the material should be wider than the damaged shingle or shingles and it should extend as high as possible to the course above.

If you must replace a broken wood shingle, extract the nails that held it, using a nail ripper. Slip the new shingle in place, then nail it and the one above it through the exposed butt ends.

Slate and Asbestos

Major damage to roofing materials such as slate, tile, and asbestos-cement shingling is uncommon. Sometimes, however, cracks will develop or a single tile will need replacement. When tackling these repairs, remember that the surfaces are more brittle (and more slippery) than other materials, and thus extra caution should be exercised.

Cracks that may develop into leaks should be sealed at once. A plastic cement compound can be used to mend the crack. If a shingle is badly damaged it will have to be replaced.

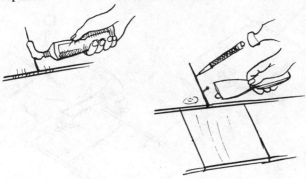

Use a hacksaw blade to cut the nails beneath a damaged shingle. It may help to break the shingle first with a few taps of the hammer. Apply a coat of roofing cement neatly onto the exposed area the shingle occupied. Slip the new shingle

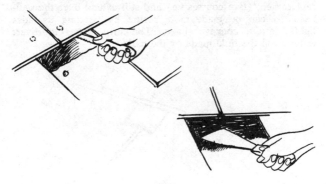

into place, then fix it by driving a single nail into the vertical joint between the shingles immediately above. Use a thin copper nail for this and place it high up on the joint.

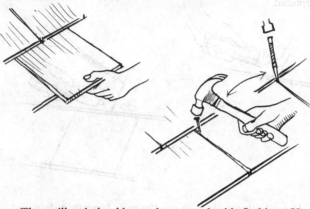

The nailhead should now be covered with flashing. You can fashion your own from a piece of galvanized iron. Cut a strip about 3 inches wide and long enough so that it can be forced up tightly under the next shingle in line with the replacement (two courses up) and still extend over the nailhead. It can be made more secure by bending its sides lightly into a concave shape. The strip serves to divert water from the hole made by the nail.

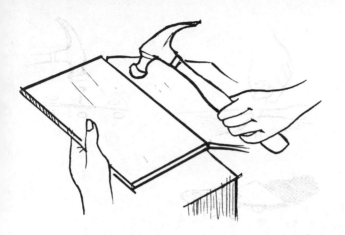

If shingle or tile must be cut to fit, lightly score the material with the point of a screwdriver or chisel first on one side, then the other. Make sure the score lines match up on both sides. Hold the shingle at an angle against the sharp edge of some solid surface and tap it with a hammer along the score, which should be resting on the sharp edge. This procedure works equally well with slate, flat tile, and asbestos-cement.

Flat Roofing

Rooftops that are flat or have only a shallow pitch to them are commonly covered with several layers of heavy felt that are cemented together with roofing asphalt. Age, together with the effects of water and sun, can blister or crack this kind of surface. If the deterioration is not widespread, you can make simple patch repairs that will prove effective.

To correct a blister, cut down the center of the fault with a sharp knife. Pack roofing asphalt into the opening, then drive some flat-head nails along both sides of the cut. This can now be covered with more asphalt and a larger patch nailed around it for further protection. The nails should be closely spaced so that the patch will not be loosened by high winds. Cover all nails with asphalt.

If a section of roof is badly blistered or otherwise damaged, with the layers beneath affected also, you can cut out the entire section and replace it with squares of new roofing felt. Cut through only one layer at a time. Place the matching pieces of new felt on dressings of fresh asphalt, tamping each layer with your feet so that it is solidly in place. Nail on a final piece that covers the entire patch; paint nailheads and seams with asphalt. Check the edges of the roofing where felt may have come unstuck. This can be nailed down and asphalt applied over the nails and seam.

Should the entire roof surface show signs of dryness, cracking, and deterioration, you will do best to recoat it.

This is not as onerous a job as it sounds. Plastic-base roofing compounds are available for just this purpose. They are simple to apply and require no special preparations other than nailing down blisters and open seams.

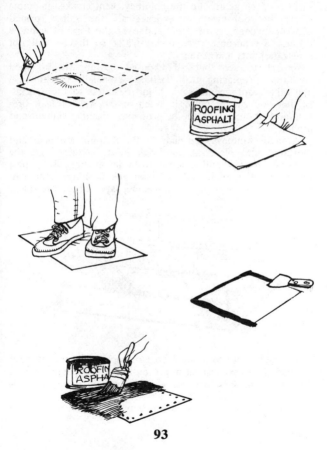

Flashing Maintenance

Made of strips or squares of galvanized metal, aluminum, or copper, flashing is used wherever the roof meets another surface—such as around the chimney, vent stacks, at points where the roof meets a vertical wall, the valley formed between two angles of roof, and over the tops of window frames. Its purpose is to divert water so that it will not penetrate joints and seams.

Inspect to see that all exposed flashing is in good condition. Replacing most flashing—especially at chimneys and other roof openings—is a job best left to the specialist, but you can accomplish much in the way of leak prevention and cures with the help of some flashing cement and asphalt.

Around chimneys, the ends of the flashing are bent and mortared into place at the brick joints. Check that the material has not pulled loose from its anchor. If it has, scrape out the joint, and remortar the flashing. You can apply a seal of asphalt to the flashing laps if they are open.

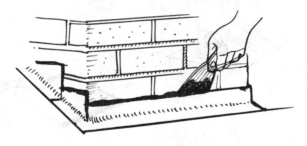

It may be wise to apply a coat of asphalt around all roof flashing anyway—just as a precaution. If appearance is a consideration, you can use a white mastic compound instead.

Valley joints and the seam between porch roofs and

higher walls are traditionally weak spots and should be
suspect if leakage is evident but no obvious damage can
be found. A solution here is to apply roofing cement to
the underside of the shingles all along the length of the
joint. If the shingles cannot be turned up at the butt, apply
the sealer instead to the shingle ends.

Gutters and Downspouts

The gutters and downspouts of your home should be
inspected at least once a year, and any adjustments or
repairs made at once. A good time to do this is in the
fall or spring—particularly if large trees adjoin the house.

Leaves, bird nests, or any other flying debris can collect in the gutters and around the downspout filters to create blockage. Damaged or missing strainers at the gutter drains can plug downspouts that empty into a dry well or sewer pipe and create damage underground.

Sweep the gutters with a hand whisk broom, removing all debris. Make sure the drain-hole strainer is intact and free. Slip-in mesh strainers can be purchased as replacements in most hardware stores. If you wish to go to the expense, you can also purchase clip-on mesh filters that will cover the open tops of the gutters. These are sold in sections and are simple to install. The side nearest the roof is slipped under the shingling; the other side clips onto the lip of the gutter.

Take a walk around the house and sight down the gutters to look for evidence of sagging. These waterways are sub-

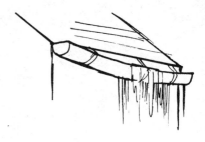

jected to a goodly amount of pressure. In the course of a year they may handle several thousand gallons of rainfall and must also bear the weight of impacted snow. It can happen that a support hanger has broken loose. Or two hangers, spaced too far apart, may have permitted a metal gutter to sag.

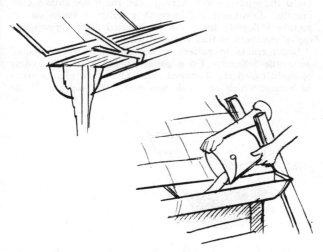

If sagging is not obvious, you can easily test for proper pitch and unimpeded flow by pouring a quantity of water into the end of the gutters away from the drain. The water should run smoothly and fully to the downspout. If it does not, note where it collects and make necessary adjustments to gutter hangers at that point and down to the outlet.

Most hangers are of two kinds. The most commonly used is the strap type, which can be bent to correct a sag. The other type is a cast hanger that is bolted to a fixed strap. Adjustments can be made by unbolting the hanger and moving it up or down to another hole in the strap.

On both types, the anchor ends are fixed by nails to the edge of the roof. Make certain they are fastened solidly, and if it is necessary to renail one, apply asphalt to nail holes and around the metal.

On a downspout that drains above the ground, blockage will be evident during the water-pouring test. If it drains under the ground into a storm sewer, run water from a hose into the downspout and observe whether it backs up. A plumber's flexible auger can be inserted down through the top of the spout to free any obstructions.

Small cracks in gutters or downspouts can be repaired with little difficulty. On a gutter, spread a smooth coating of asphalt over the damaged area. Over this, place a piece of burlap, which you will then paint with asphalt. If the

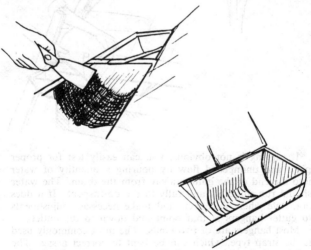

crack is large, or a section of the gutter is weakened by corrosion, cut and bend to shape a piece of aluminum that can be crimped into place at both lips of the gutter. The piece should be laid over asphalt, and the seams smoothly sealed with the same compound. Small cracks and holes in downspouts can be plugged with a dab of asphalt. If damage or corrosion is extensive in either gutters or downspouts, it is best to replace entire sections.

Long-time protection of the gutters can be obtained by painting the insides with a thin coating of asphalt.

Where downspouts empty directly onto the ground, drainage problems may arise. Puddles collect, and water may seep through the ground to attack the foundation (see Chapter 2). The simplest solution to this problem is to install a splash guard beneath the downspout. (Plastic ones are available, or a concrete pad can be built.) Make sure that it carries the water at least 4 feet away from the foundation.

CHAPTER 6

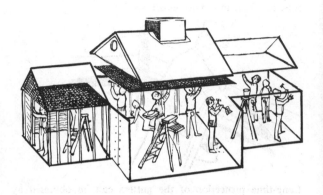

Interior Walls
and Ceilings

Every homeowner is faced, at some time or another, with the problem of correcting damage to his ceilings and walls. The trouble could be loose, broken, or bulging plaster as the result of water leakage. Cracks may reappear after they have been plastered over. Surface stains must be dealt with.

Perhaps an entire section of wall or ceiling looks as if it needs replastering—or would a plasterboard patch carefully applied do the job just as well?

To preserve the beauty of your home's interior (and to

maintain its value overall) you should be prepared to handle such repair work quickly and efficiently.

Fortunately, the tools and materials needed for these jobs are on hand or are cheaply and easily available. With an understanding of some of the skills involved you can tackle resurfacing of old walls and ceilings with wallboard or any of the many types of tiles now on the market.

Plaster Repairs

Plaster on ceilings and walls is generally applied over a lathing of wood, metal, or gypsum, the latter most common except in older homes. This lathing serves as a foundation for the plaster and is in turn fixed to the framework behind it.

Small cracks and holes in plaster can be filled with spackling compound, which is available either in dry or premixed form. First clear away all loose plaster and dust. Work the spackle tightly into the opening with a flexible putty knife. Trim the excess flush with the wall, wiping with the knife in alternate crisscross strokes. Give the compound plenty of time to dry, then sand the area smooth, using medium sandpaper.

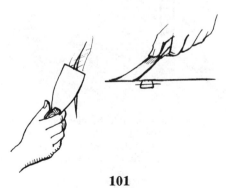

When cracks are long and deep, or the sides of a smaller crack appear weak, you will have to cut back the edges of the crack with a pointed tool until you reach firm material. It is best if you can undercut the sides so that they are wider at the bottom than at the top. This will provide a stronger bond when the compound sets.

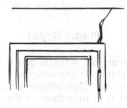

Troublesome cracks of this sort are usually found around window and door frames and at the junctions of wall and ceiling. They are mostly caused by structural stresses; when they first appear in a newer home, it is a sign that the foundation is settling—a normal occurrence if damage is not severe.

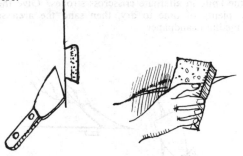

Should a larger crack or hole be cleaned out to a point where the lathing behind it is exposed, you should apply the patching compound in two layers to avoid shrinking problems. The first layer should come to within ⅛ inch of the surface. Permit it to dry, then apply the second layer. If the damaged area is wide, a trowel will do a better job than the putty knife. Wetting down the sides and surrounding plaster of the gap before you apply the compound will aid in minimizing shrinkage.

If water damage has caused plaster to peel and flake, it may be necessary to repair a large section of ceiling or wall. This also applies where the plaster appears to bulge, suggesting that it has broken away from the lathing, or that the lathing has come loose.

First knock out the damaged plaster with a hammer. Keep a check on the blows so that no further damage is done to lathing. Remove plaster until you have reached material that is firmly anchored. For simplicity's sake, fashion the opening into a square or rectangle. Use a chisel or other sharp instrument to undercut the edges of the plaster on all four sides.

If the lathing has pulled loose, renail it firmly to the studs before proceeding with the repair. If the lathing is damaged,

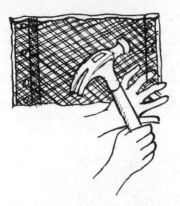

cut it back to the studs on either side and remove damaged sections. Replace it with new lath or plasterboard, nailing it firmly to the studs.

Wet the lath and surrounding plaster, then trowel on a smooth coating of patching plaster, to within $\frac{1}{16}$ inch of the surface. Make sure to pack it thoroughly into the crevice

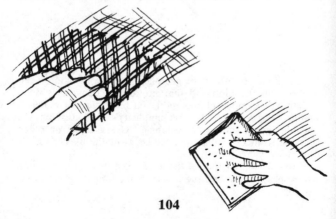

between patch and wall. Scratch the surface slightly to provide "tooth" for the finish coat, then allow to dry. Trowel on a final coat, smoothing it over. When dry, sand smooth with surrounding plaster.

When a plaster wall is covered with "map" or shrinkage cracks, about the only solution short of replastering or covering with a new material is to paint it over with one of the textured paints available on the market. These paints are extremely thick and will often cover such irregularities successfully.

Gypsum Wallboard

Gypsum wallboard is a surfacing material commonly used for both walls and ceilings. Also known as plasterboard and sheetrock, it is made of compressed gypsum plaster between two sheets of heavy paper or cardboard. The sheets range in sizes up to 4' by 16', though 4' by 8' is most favored by builders, and come in thicknesses of ⅜ inch and ½ inch.

Wallboard is usually nailed, or cemented and nailed, directly to the studs. The board is subject to dents, such as may be caused by the sharp corner of a piece of furniture. Depressions of this sort can be corrected quickly with spackling compound or a special gypsum cement. Nail holes can also be filled in this fashion also. No preparation of the surface is necessary, and the compound can be smoothed with sandpaper once it dries.

Settling of the house's foundation, or the use of green wood for backing supports, can result in a vertical warping of the plasterboard. When this happens, the nails that hold the panel in place may "pop" loose. This can be corrected by removing the loosened nail and driving a single nail just above or below the old nail hole, at the same time pushing the board firmly to hold it in place. Use only a screw-type nail for the fastening, and hammer it

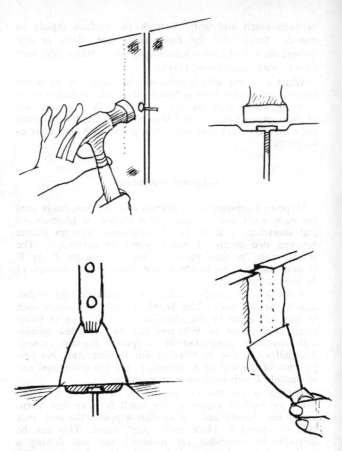

carefully so that a shallow depression is formed around the nailhead. Patch and finish the repair with spackling compound.

106

The joints between panels are closed with gypsum cement and a special reinforcing tape. To close a seam that has broken open, first clean out the seam with a sharp-pointed tool (a beer-can opener does a good job). Pull or scrape away remnants of the old tape, then sand the seam to prepare the surface. The area you have sanded should be slightly wider than the replacement tape.

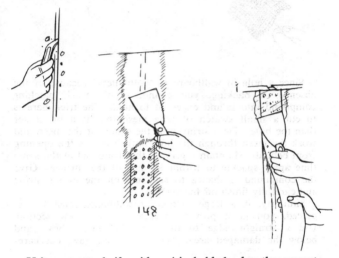

Using a putty knife with a 4-inch blade, lay the cement smoothly and evenly into the seam and around it. Before the cement has had a chance to dry, apply the tape over the seam, centering it and removing all wrinkles and air bubbles with the blade of the knife. Now apply more cement over the tape. Work it on smoothly and remove all excess. After it dries, sand it smooth and "feather" both sides of the tape. To provide a smoother finish, it may be necessary to apply another coat of cement and repeat the sanding.

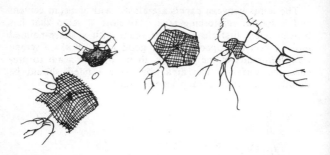

Since a hole in wallboard is "bottomless" because of the absence of backing, you cannot simply work patching compound into it and expect it to hold. The trick here is to cut a small swatch of wire mesh that is a bit larger than the hole. Tie a string near the center of the mesh and work the mesh through the hole until it covers the opening from behind. Maintain a grip on the string and at the same time apply spackle to within ⅛ inch of the surface. Give the compound a chance to set, snip off the excess string and carefully finish off the surface.

Similarly, if a large section of wallboard must be replaced, you must provide backing for the new section. Use a straight edge to draw parallel lines above and below the damaged area. With a keyhole saw, cut care-

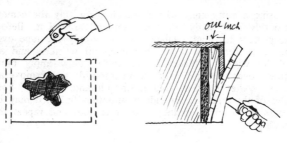

fully along the lines until you encounter the studs on either side of the damage. Cut another inch of wallboard so that you are over the center line of the stud. Now cut straight down along this line on both studs.

If the damaged area extends beyond the width of two studs, it is best to continue the horizontal cut to the next stud.

Measure the size of the opening and cut a new piece of board to fit. You do not have to use a saw: use a sharp knife to score the face of the board. Snap it over a straightedge or the edge of a table, then score the rear to break it off cleanly. The new section can be nailed directly to the studs, but first you must provide horizontal backing because of the horizontal seams. Use sections of 2-x-4- or 2-x-3-inch lumber, sawing them to size so they can be toenailed to the studs. One support for the top and bottom of the replacement section will suffice. Nail the section into place and finish the seams as described above.

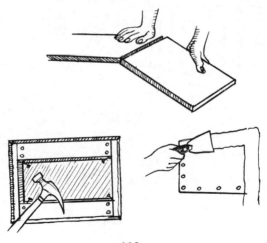

Wall Paneling

Unsightly wall surfaces can be refinished with paneling of your choice, such as wallboard, plywood, fiberboard, or hardboard, which comes in various finishes and requires no further covering. Or you may decide to panel a wall with wood. It all depends on the application and how much you wish to spend.

In all cases, though, you will have to provide a base to support the new material. This is done with furring strips, lengths of 1-x-2-inch wood that can be purchased by the bundle at your local lumberyard.

To apply furring to a plaster wall, the strips must be placed horizontally and nailed to the wall studs. Spacing is usually 16 inches on center. Some types of paneling also require vertical furring strips where two panels meet; follow manufacturer's recommendations in this regard. The

Firring with
16 inch centers

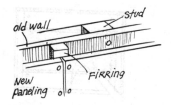

old wall

stud

New paneling

Firring

baseboard along the bottom of the wall should be removed, as well as any molding and trim. Openings in the wall, such as windows and doors, should be surrounded by furring strips. A long straight-edge board can be used to detect bulges or depressions between wall and the outside of the furring strips. A depression can be corrected by placing wood shims behind the strip to bring it in line with the others. A bulge is handled by planing the surface of the strip. Make these checks accurately, for any variances will show only too plainly when the paneling is nailed into place.

For walls of concrete, the furring can be nailed directly onto the concrete, using special masonry nails. If the surface of a masonry wall is extremely irregular along its face, you should first nail up a framework of 2-x-2-inch lumber, shimming where necessary to even it up. Apply the furring over this.

When working with large sheets of light, flexible paneling, it is best to do your nailing from the center out to the sides. This will avoid any buckling problem. When measuring how much paneling you will need to cover the area, allow 10 percent extra for waste.

Ceramic Tile Repair

Ceramic tile is easily set in place with a white, waterproof tile caulking used to fill the spaces around the tile. These same adhesive compounds can be used to make repairs on ceramic tile that has been cemented with Portland cement, the old method of fastening.

As soon as a tile comes loose or cracks, it should be replaced with a new one. Use a chisel to cut around the damaged tile. Try not to damage the surrounding tiles. If the original fastening is cement, you will have to chisel

111

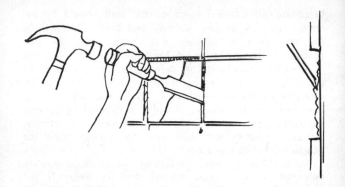

away a part of the cement so the replacement tile will not extend beyond the surface of surrounding tiles.

Apply a generous bead of cement to the back of the new tile, then press it into place firmly. Wipe off all excess cement immediately. To hold the tile in place until the cement sets, you can either drive small wood wedges into the joints or support it with strips of masking tape. There should be an even space all around the tile. When the cement dries, remove the supports and fill the joints with white compound.

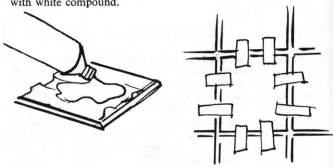

To cut ceramic tile to fit you must use a glass cutter. Make a score along a guide line on the face of the tile, then place the tile over a nail and apply pressure on both sides to snap it clean. A file or emery cloth can be used to smooth the edges of the cut. For a curved cut, score the guide line, then make crisscross scores inside the area of the cut. Use a pliers to break out the scored section little by little.

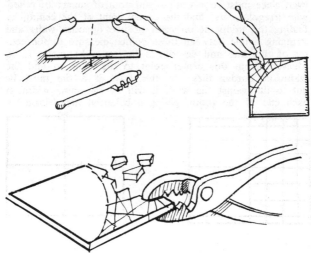

When small, fine cracks appear in ceramic tile there is no cure but replacement. Shrinkage cracks around the wall of tile can be filled with white plastic compound sold for that purpose. Correct such cracks as soon as they appear to prevent splash water or condensation from ruining the wall interior. Tile surfaces should never be cleaned with an abrasive agent. Warm water and a detergent is best (soap leaves a film).

Ceiling Tile

Tiles are an excellent choice for many ceiling resurfacing jobs. Acoustical tile is especially popular, easy to work with, and can do much to brighten up a ceiling. It comes in a wide variety of patterns to suit just about any decor.

Ceiling tile installation is begun at a room corner. However, since most rooms are slightly out of square or otherwise irregular, first find the center point of the ceiling by finding the midpoint on each of two opposite walls and stringing a line between these points; measure to the center of this line and describe a line at right angles to it. Measure from this center point to the walls to find the width of border tiles. In this way, if a tile must be cut to fit against the wall, it will be the same width at each end of the room, giving a balanced appearance.

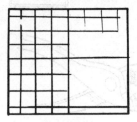
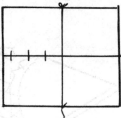

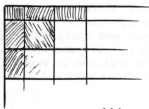

114

If an existing ceiling is level and in sound condition, ceiling tiles can be applied right over it with adhesive. Make sure the ceiling is clean and free of grease and water-soluble paint. Dab adhesive on the back of each tile in four or five spots and place it against the ceiling in approximate position, then slide it into place, spreading the mastic. Slight depressions in the ceiling can be reconciled by applying a thicker coating of adhesive.

Where the existing ceiling is badly cracked or peeling, and in basements, attics, and other areas where the joists or rafters are exposed, the best method of installing ceiling tiles is by stapling them to furring strips. Place the first strip against the wall, nailing securely to each joist. The placement of the second strip depends upon the width you have determined for the border tiles. All other strips are placed on 12-inch centers (or whatever other width tiles you may be using). Where pipes and cables are hung below the joists, a double layer of furring strips may be used to clear these obstructions. In this case, the first layer may be spaced on about 24-inch centers (more or less depending on where the obstructions fall). Pipes that are several inches below the joists should be boxed with furring strips. It is good insurance to make a sketch of your plumbing system, including the location of valves, before enclosure so that a minimum number of tiles need be removed if you ever require access to the pipes.

The furring strips should be checked with a level and shimmed with wood wedges where necessary to provide

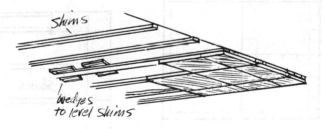

115

an even, level backing for the tiles. Snap a chalk line across the furring strips as a guideline for border tiles. Measure and cut each border tile individually to assure an accurate fit. (When measuring, do not include tongues and flanges.) Cut the tiles face up with a sharp fiber-board knife. Fit the first tile in the corner, carefully align-ing it with the two intersecting guidelines; staple it secure-ly through the flanges. Install the border tiles adjacent to the corner tile, then install another border tile along each wall and begin filling in between the border tiles with full tiles, working across the ceiling. Make certain that each tile is butted tightly to and aligned properly with its neighbors before stapling. Wherever possible, light fix-tures, vents, and other ceiling fittings should be positioned between furring strips so they will fall in the center of a

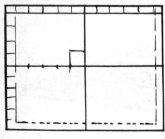

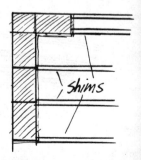

shims

single tile, minimizing cutting and fitting. When you reach the borders on the opposite side of the room, the final tiles will be face-nailed to the furring strips. A cove or crown molding at the joint between walls and ceiling will conceal the nails.

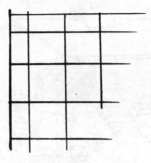

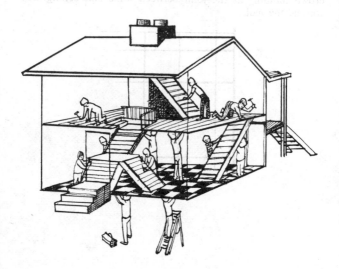

CHAPTER 7

Floors and Stairs

High on the list of priority items in the maintenance of your home's interior is the care and repair of floors and stairs. Squeaks, creaks, and groans may need correcting, not only because they are annoying, but also because they may signal the beginning of deterioration.

Sometimes there is more than just appearance at stake; there may also be a strong aspect of safety involved. Loose or worn floorboards and stair treads are hazardous.

A sagging floor may indicate a weakening of the floor's understructure. Few homeowners realize that age, the settling of the foundation, the shifting or addition of heavy loads, and perhaps poorly planned renovations of rooms can create stresses to the beams and joists that support the flooring. Caught in time, many of these problems can be handled by the homeowner before they demand a thorough overhaul, which would necessitate calling in outside help.

Often an old floor can be corrected and made like new with only some simple labor on your part. Resilient floor coverings such as linoleum, vinyl, or tile can be installed, or the existing surface material can be repaired, at relatively little cost. A concrete flooring may betray the effects of poor workmanship or corrosion—you should be familiar with the signs and know how to go about repairing the damage or stopping it in its tracks.

Wood Floor Repairs

Why live with a floor that complains all the time? Elimination of squeaks and creaks can be managed with relatively little effort, the means depending on the floor's construction and whether the subflooring is accessible from below.

Most wood floors consist of two layers: a subfloor of boards or plywood and the finished floor of narrower boards—usually hardwood—tongued and grooved together and nailed into place. The subflooring is supported from

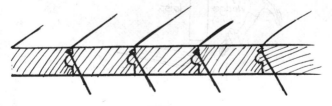

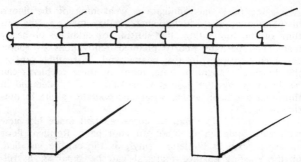

underneath by wood joists normally spaced on 16-inch centers. A squeak is usually the result of a board or boards having separated from what is beneath. The finish floor may have pulled away from the subfloor, or the subfloor may have warped or sagged and pulled away from the joists.

It is best to make your inspection and repairs from under the floor, if this is not concealed by a ceiling or other barrier. Have someone walk around overhead so that you can pinpoint the problem. Inspect the area around the squeak. Make sure joists are level and check between joists and subflooring for signs of warping or lifting of the floor boards.

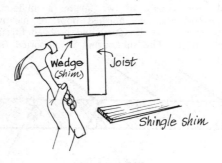

Wedge (shim)

Joist

Shingle shim

If a squeak is detected directly over a joist, an effective method of quieting it is to drive thin wood shims between the joist and subflooring. Pieces of shingle are ideal for this. Hammer them into place over one or more joists, as necessary. Larger wedges of wood can be used if needed.

When the squeak originates between joists, first install a header of 2 x 4 or 2 x 6 lumber to act as a base for the shimming. Cut the header so that it fits snugly between two joists. Tap it up firmly against the subfloor, narrow side up, and toenail it securely in place. Now work in shims as needed between header and subfloor. This should eliminate the noise.

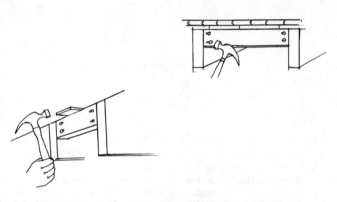

Another approach is to drive a screw up through the subfloor and into the finish floor where the squeak is found. Use a wood screw about 1 inch long for this operation—enough to penetrate the subfloor but not the finish floor, and have someone stand on the floor overhead. It is best to drill a pilot hole to help start the screw, and to avoid splitting the hardwood floor. Again,

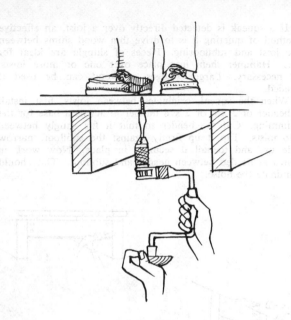

be careful not to penetrate the finish floor. Maintain the weight overhead as you drive the screw so that subfloor and finish floor will be brought together.

These methods cannot be used if the understructure is inaccessible. In that case, you will have to make the repairs from topside. You can often silence a squeak by working some talcum powder or powdered stainless lubricant into the cracks between floorboards but this is only a temporary treatment. The best way is to nail the noisy board.

Use long finishing nails for this job. Drive them in pairs, as required, along or across the board. The nails should be driven at an angle, each pair forming a V, the

122

point of which would meet under the subfloor. Drill pilot holes to avoid splitting the hardwood. Use a nail set to recess nailheads. The holes can be filled with putty or plugged with wax patching crayon. If you are doing this kind of work on a floor that is covered with linoleum or tile, about the only thing you can do is nail right through the floor covering. There is a lot of guesswork involved here because the boards are unseen, so prod around with your foot to try to pinpoint the squeak as best as possible. This will avoid your having to drive too many nails. The holes in the covering can be plugged with wax crayon.

Cracked and Split Flooring

Floorboards become damaged for a variety of reasons, the most common of which are shrinkage and expansion because of exposure to water. When wet, the boards expand against their joints. As they dry they return to their former size, causing cracks to appear either between the joints or along the grain of the board. New floors laid with green or wet wood will also produce cracks.

123

You should make it a rule never to wash a wood floor with water. Rather, treat the wood with an application of any of the floor sealers available, then give it a good waxing for an easy-to-maintain protective finish.

Cracks can be filled with a variety of compounds. You can use a mixture of glue and sawdust, a wood-fiber putty, or plastic wood. The compound is pressed into the crack and then sanded and stained to the proper color.

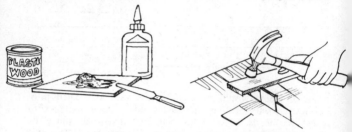

You can also fashion small wedges of hardwood to fill the crack, hammering them in tightly, then planing the excess.

Splits along the grain of a board should be filled with a mixture of glue and sawdust. This will prevent the board from splitting further.

A warped board can sometimes be evened off with a good sanding or by planing. First make sure all nail-heads have been recessed. If the board is a wide one,

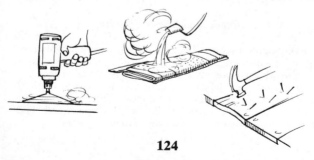

you can also try to flatten it by soaking it with water then nailing it flat. Otherwise it will have to be replaced with a new board.

To remove a badly worn or damaged section of board, first drill large holes at each end of the damaged section. The holes should not extend through the subfloor below. Drill close to the edges of the board, then carefully chisel out the damaged section across and along its grain, taking care not to harm the tongue and groove sides of the adjoining boards. Cut the replacement piece to size. Using your chisel, remove the bottom half of the groove on the replacement piece. You can now slip the new board into place, nail it down, recessing the nailheads, and plane it flush, if necessary.

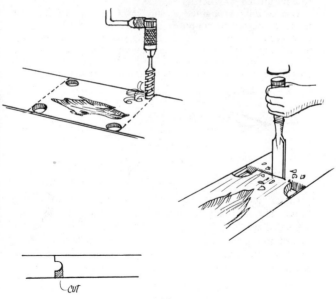

Sagging Floors

When a floor sags at any point or feels bouncy when you walk over it, part of the understructure is probably weak. This presents a potentially dangerous condition that should be corrected without delay. Because the condition usually is found at the lower floors of the house, thereby providing you with ready access to the understructure, you can often make the necessary repairs and adjustments yourself.

The cause of the sagging may be that the joists are spaced too far apart to provide rigid support for weakened subflooring. One or more joists may have warped or sagged. The beam that supports the joists may not be making contact all the way across.

Use a long straightedge and level to inspect the subflooring, joists, and supporting beams. If a joist has warped or sagged, but is otherwise sound, you can raise the floor by driving hardwood wedges between the joist and subflooring. Additional support is gained by toenailing a sturdy crosspiece between the joists under the raised floor.

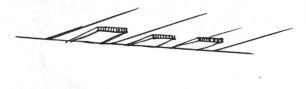

Check to see that all joists are resting on the main beam. It often happens that a beam will sag at the center —particularly if it is made of wood. Support posts may be spaced too far apart, or they may have buckled or rotted or sunk into the concrete floor. Or they may be absent altogether, in which case you will have to add one or more.

Adjustable metal posts that have a screw-type jack at the end can be used to raise the beam into position. These can be left in place as permanent supports, if needed. Obviously, the base of the jack must rest on a solid cement footing. If the cement floor is less than 4 inches thick or shows signs of deterioration, you must put in a new footing.

Because of potential damage to the frame and walls of the house, you must never attempt to raise the beam more than a slight amount at a time. Put the jack post into position under the beam so that it just touches. Make sure the jack is perfectly vertical, then give the screw a half turn and stop. Wait several days to a week, then give it another half turn. Do not be in a hurry—chances are it took quite a while for the beam to sag that much, so it can wait to be straightened out. Continue a little at a time until the floor overhead is level, then either insert a chock between the existing post and the beam or leave the jack post in position permanently.

You can check the level of the floor with a long straightedge as you go along. Or you can tack a string from wall to wall across the floor above the sag. If the string is kept taut, you will be able to observe the distance between it and the floor as this distance gradually diminishes.

Concrete Flooring

Smooth-finish concrete flooring is durable and normally requires little maintenance. However, trouble can sometimes arise, generally as the result of poor workmanship. Because of its porosity, new concrete should be treated with an application of penetrating varnish or paint sealer. A paste-wax coating can be added for further protection.

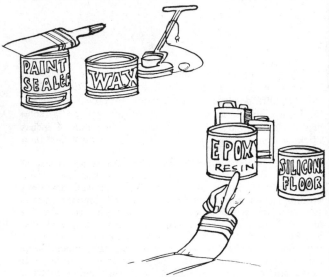

Concrete sealer paints can also be applied to correct pitted and dusty concrete, two common problems (see Chapter 2). These paints come in clear form and in colors with silicone, epoxy-resin, or latex bases, the last a good choice for rooms that experience occasional dampness. It is usually necessary to apply more than one coat of paint—the first to seal and the following to fill.

Keep an eye out for damp spots on slab floors that have heating or water pipes imbedded in the concrete; this may indicate a leak in the pipes and the need to call in professional help. Simple cracks can be filled easily enough with patching compound, then treated as described previously. If a floor is badly damaged, however, you will have to lay in a reinforced topping of concrete (refer to section on basement floors, Chapter 2). An unsightly floor that is still sound can be prepared to receive a covering of tile or linoleum.

Linoleum and Tile

Resilient floor coverings laid over wood and concrete are cemented in place with an adhesive such as mastic. Kept waxed and clean they wear well, but after a time it will become necessary to replace one or more damaged tiles or deal with worn or broken linoleum. A tile or linoleum seam may come unstuck, in which case a recementing job is needed.

Finding a replacement floor tile that will match the rest is not always easy. Manufacturers of tile recommend that extra units be purchased with the original floor, not only to allow for wastage during installation, but to provide for just this contingency. If you are really stuck with a floor pattern, style, or color that is not available, a possible solution would be to remove several good tiles and install new ones that will create a limited pattern or decorative path encompassing the damaged area. Of course you should first check with your dealer to see whether the tile is available through the manufacturer. Take along a sample.

Tiles are laid butted tightly against each other, and removal of one, if not done carefully, can cause damage to others. To make the job easier, the cement and the tile can first be softened by heat. The professionals have special "hot plates" for this purpose, but you can do the

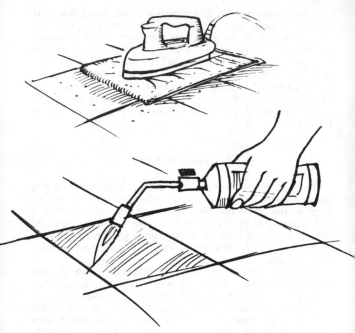

job almost as effectively with a household electric iron. Set it to its hottest and put a damp cloth between it and the tile. A blowtorch played over the center of the tile is a faster method, but the flame should not come in direct contact with the tile.

While the tile is still hot, work the tip of a putty knife under a raised corner or seam and carefully pry loose the tile. If it does not come easily—or if you are unable to use heat because of the tile's composition—you may have to cut out the tile in pieces with a hammer and chisel, taking care not to gouge the subfloor. Begin this operation by first cutting into the seam around the tile with a sharp knife. As you remove the tile with the chisel, work from the center out to the edges; this minimizes the possibility of damage to surrounding tiles.

Sometimes, if the damaged tile is removed in one piece by the heating method, the cement will be tacky enough so that you can simply press a new tile in its place. Otherwise, the old cement should be scraped off to provide a smooth base, then new cement put down. Apply it evenly and sparingly to avoid its squeezing up around the edges of the tile.

On linoleum and sheet vinyl, a seam may lift because the cement was not applied properly, or has been weakened by water. This can be corrected by applying fresh cement to the area beneath the flooring material and placing a heavy object on top until it dries. Work the cement in with a flexible blade, taking care not to tear the material.

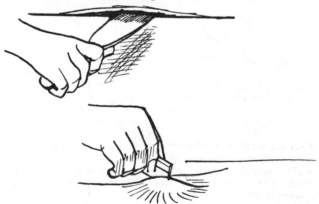

Wipe off the excess and allow plenty of time to dry. If there is a bubble or raised spot remote from a seam, slit the raised portion along its length with a razor or sharp knife and work the cement under the lifted areas.

You can renew worn or grubby looking linoleum, if it is otherwise intact, by giving it a couple coats of floor enamel in a color of your choice. First prepare the floor by removing all traces of wax or grease; steel wool and alcohol will help here. When it is clean and dry, apply a first coat of paint. When that is dry, give it a finish coat. You can add more colors to provide a stipple effect, or to create a pattern laid out with masking tape. The floor should then be waxed.

Broken linoleum can be repaired with a patch of new material. Lay the new linoleum over the damaged surface and cut through both new and old linoleum with a sharp knife. A straightedge will help guide the cut. The material is more flexible and will lay flat better if it is warm. Remove the old piece and check the fit of the cut patch.

Cut through new and old
linoleum at same time

Trim 1/16 off
all around

Trim the surrounding linoleum so that there is a 1/16-inch gap all around—this will fill in later when the new piece swells naturally. Apply cement and press the patch in place. The seams can be tapped flush with a mallet or a hammer and a block of wood.

Linoleum and tile can be applied over any wood or concrete floor (above grade) that is in good condition. In tile you have a choice of vinyl, cork, linoleum, rubber, vinyl asbestos, or asphalt, the last two preferred for concrete that comes in direct contact with the ground.

Before tile can be put down, you will have to correct any irregularities in the floor. Make sure nailheads do not protrude. Sand or plane smooth any raised surfaces and eliminate any existing squeaks. If it is a concrete floor, fill any cracks or gouges.

Keep in mind that resilient tiles of any composition will conform to the shape of the surface they cover. If the floor is uneven, broken, badly scarred, or pitted, you will have to lay in a hard, flat foundation for the tiles. This layer can be of hardboard or plywood, and it is nailed directly to the existing flooring. If a concrete floor is subject to persistent dampness, condensation, or leakage, you will have to correct this before proceeding any further, either by laying a waterproof barrier or pouring a new topping.

Tile can be applied successfully by the homeowner, but the directions supplied by the manufacturer must be followed to the letter. Otherwise the results can be disappointing. Your dealer can advise you as to the number of tiles you will need to cover a given area and also any specific recommendations for the make or type of tile. When laying linoleum, first make a pattern out of taped-together newspaper or heavy wrapping paper, using small pieces for fit around corners and obstructions. Use this to trace an outline on the underside of the linoleum (remembering to turn the pattern over). It is a quick, simple step that can prevent a lot of aggravation.

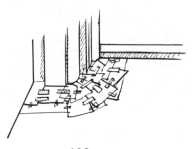

Stair Repairs

A stair consists of three parts: tread, riser, and stringer. On some stairs the tread rests on the riser in a simple butt joint of glue and nails, in others a tongue-and-rabbet joint, or dado is used. The stringers or side pieces serve to support the treads.

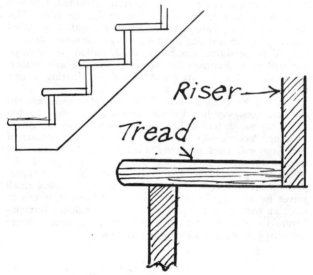

When squeaks occur, it is because the tread or riser has worked loose at some point. If the treads are attached by butt joints (you can check this by prying off a part of the molding under the nose of the tread), you can tighten the tread by renailing it to the top of the riser. Have someone stand on the tread during the operation. Drive finishing nails at angles through the top of the tread into the center of the riser top. The holes can be filled

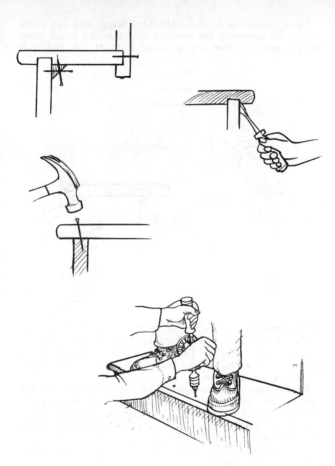

with wood putty. If the tread is made of hardwood, you can avoid splits and bent nails by first drilling pilot holes.

On a dadoed or tongue-and-rabbet setup, you can avoid nailing by removing the molding and working small glued wedges into the side of the tread slot. If the underside

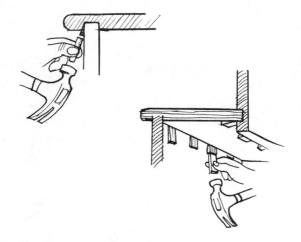

of the stairway is accessible, apply the wedges from behind. While under there, check for any loose wedges between the tread and stringer. Tighten these or replace them, as necessary. Nail the bottom ends of the riser to the tread, if this has worked loose.

Replacement of a damaged or broken tread is a job that usually calls for the services of a carpenter. However, if the wall end of the tread butts against the stringer, rather than being recessed into it, the job is considerably easier and you may wish to tackle it.

First remove all molding from under the tread nosing. The feet of the balusters may be toenailed to the top of the tread or glued into slots. In such cases, use a hacksaw blade to sever the balusters as close to the tread as possible, exercising care to limit damage while cutting. The tops of the balusters are usually held in place with glue and can be separated from the anchor by twisting.

Hammer carefully under the nosing of the tread until there is a gap between the tread and riser. A pry bar may help here. Depending on the construction of the stair, you can continue prying until the tread can be worked loose by hand, or cut the nails that hold it with a hacksaw. The tread can now be used as a pattern for the new step. Or, if wear is the only problem, it may be possible to turn over and use the other side instead. Fasten the tread with glue and nails; fill the nail holes with wood putty.

CHAPTER 8

Doors and Windows

A door or window sticks. The door scrapes the flooring thin when it is opened. A window pane cracks or breaks. A sash cord needs replacement. You have to put your shoulder to the door to latch it shut. Window or door screens need patching or renewing. And so on—it happens in the best of homes!

The needed repairs can be frustrating, ruinous even, if tackled haphazardly. Or they can be simple and economical. The door problem may be the result of faulty installation, or the door may have become warped or swollen by humidity. The frame itself may be twisted out of shape. Sometimes you will have to remove or rebuild material to correct the problem. But more often than not it can be handled with some hinge adjustments.

There is also a right way and a wrong way to approach window problems. Using the wrong tool or method can cause further damage or waste time. In just a few steps, you can replace window panes yourself without having to call a glazier.

Doors That Stick

A door swells when it is damp and becomes difficult to operate. But before you attempt to plane off the door rails (ends) or stiles (sides) it is wise to remember that the wood will shrink as the air dries out. Think twice before planing if you suspect that this is only a cyclical condition.

The first thing to check is the condition of the hinges. Position yourself on the side of the door opposite the stops (so that it closes *away* from you). With the door closed examine the spaces between the door and frame. You can run a sheet of paper around the edges to observe the hang of the door; where it binds, the door is too tight. If

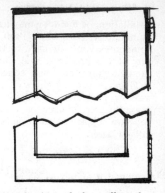

there is a space at the top, latch side of the rail and a corresponding space at the bottom, hinge side, it means that the upper hinge is probably loose, perhaps the lower one as well.

Open the door to expose the hinges. Relieve pressure on the top hinge by having someone lightly support the door by its handle, or by slipping a wedge of some sort under the bottom rail. Use a broad-bladed screwdriver to tighten all the screws. If a screw does not appear to have any purchase, the wood around the screw has deteriorated. This can be corrected.

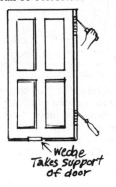

wedge
Takes support
of door

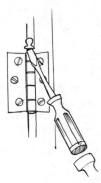

140

Remove the door by knocking out first the lower, then the upper hinge pin. Use a screwdriver angled so that the head of the pin is driven up and out. Should the pin be frozen, remove the hinge at the jamb. Inspect the mortise and the condition of the wood. If the holes look pulpy or rotted, hammer in a small wooden plug coated with glue or stuff the spaces with toothpicks or wooden matches dipped in glue. Trim, then replace the hinge and rescrew, using longer screws if possible.

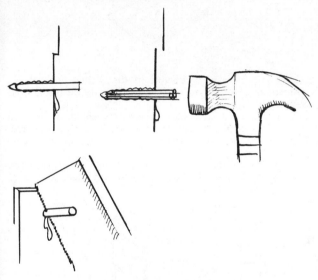

The difficulty may be that the hinge plate is not recessed deeply enough in the mortise, in which case you will have to chisel the mortise deeper. Or it may be possible, if spacing at the latch stile permits, to build up the lower hinge and thus shift the door to the vertical. The shim

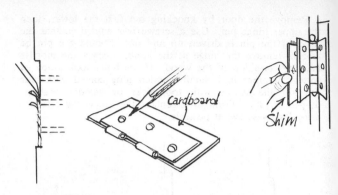

can be any piece of cardboard of the correct thickness (a matchbook cover serves well) and it should fill the mortise completely.

When the door binds along the entire length of the latch stile, you will have to cut the mortises deeper, as required. If necessary, you can deepen the mortises on the jamb and the door.

Shimming will help if the door tends to spring open when you try to close it. In this case you will place a strip of

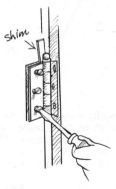

142

cardboard only behind half the width of the hinge leaf. You do not have to remove the hinge for this operation. Loosen the screws so that when the door is partially closed, the hinge leaf comes away from the mortise. Slip the shim into this space and tighten the screws. Shimming at this point serves to change the angle of the door so that it leans toward the outside stop.

If the hinge stile is catching or binding along the stop you can reposition the hinge leaf in its mortise to pull the door away a bit.

Fitting the Door

Often a door is binding at several points at once because it or the frame has been warped out of shape. (Cracks or stress marks on the plaster around the frame are signs that the frame is at fault.) In either case, adjusting the fit of the hinges will not do the job completely. You will have to plane or sand the door as well.

Your inspection will show where excess material has to be removed. Usually only a part of a side has to be touched up, rather than the entire length of a stile or rail. If such is the case at the outside stile you can probably get away without having to remove the door.

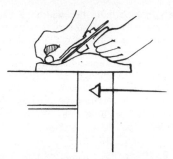

Mark off the sticking areas while the door is closed so you will know how much has to be cut. Remove the door and prop it on its side against some solid support. Work the plane in smooth strokes and do not bite too deeply at any one time. If the binding exists at the latch area of the door it may prove simpler to plane the hinge side instead. Hinge leaves are easier to remove than the lock assembly.

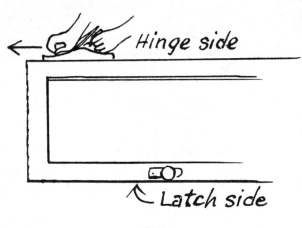

Hinge side

Latch side

When the door rubs at the top or bottom, you will have to plane one or both rails, either partially or fully. Keep in mind that you will be cutting across the grain, and if you work too roughly or use a dull tool it is easy to splinter the wood. If the amount to be removed is fractional, try a sanding block instead, but take care not to bevel the door edges.

A door sometimes becomes too narrow because of shrinkage, with the result that the latch is not able to reach the striker plate to engage it. If the distance is small, you can correct this by removing the striker plate and bringing it closer to the door with a wood shim.

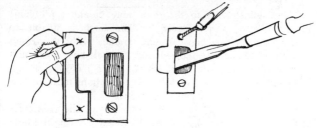

When the space to be filled is much wider, however, the best solution is to build up the width of the door by cementing and nailing a strip of wood along the hinge stile. The strip should be wide enough to close the gap and as

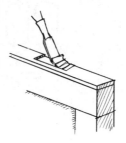

thick as the stile. Measure to determine where the hinge leaves should be set and chisel new mortises to receive them. The strip can be finished to match the door.

These adjustments to the door may create a problem: the door now swings freely but the latch is unable to engage the striker plate in the frame, with the result that the plate must be repositioned. To tell how much and in what direction, rub some crayon over the face of the striker plate and close the door. The resultant mark on the plate will indicate what has to be done.

If the latch is centered, but falls short of the receptacle in the plate, you might try filing the metal to bring the hole closer. Trim wood from the mortise, if required. If the

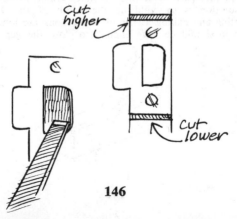

Cut higher

Cut lower

entire plate has to be moved, fill the original screw holes with plugs before attempting to screw the plate in a new position. Gaps between the plate and the mortise can be filled with wood putty and touched up with paint. These same instructions apply when the plate must be moved up or down to meet the latch.

Window Problems

When a wood window sash sticks or binds, it is usually because paint has worked into the sash molding or because the sash or frame has become swollen.

Paint-stuck windows can sometimes be freed by tapping along both sides of the sash with a hammer and block of wood. If this does not free the window, insert the blade

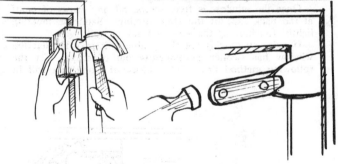

of a paint scraper or a broad, thin chisel between the sash and the stop molding. Tap the blade in with a hammer then rock the tool back and forth gently to force the sash back from the molding. Repeat this at several points at each side of the sash until it can move freely. Never use a screwdriver for this job, as it will only gouge the wood.

If the sticking is severe, or if a seal forms at the bottom edge of the sash after a new paint job, the window can be pried loose from the outside without damage to the

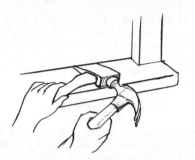

finish. A hatchet is a good tool for this, or any broad, hard metal wedge. Hammer the tool along the bottom of the sash and pry as you go along.

Once the window is free, scrape off any crusts of paint at the back face of the stop molding. Sand the molding lightly, touching up the window track as well.

If paint sticking is not the problem, it may be that the window has swollen permanently out of shape. Try the following method first: Cut a block of wood that will fit

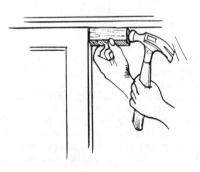

snugly into the channel between the inside and outside window stops. Give the block several smart raps with a hammer at both sides of the window. This should free the sash so that it can be raised at least partially. Repeat the procedure at the exposed channels at the bottom. A lubricant such as paraffin or candle wax may then be applied to the channels.

If this method fails the sash will have to be removed from the frame to make the necessary adjustments. (In order to remove the top sash the bottom one must come out first.) Most modern windows are equipped with metal tension strips fastened to the channels. With this kind it may be possible to remove the sash simply by pressing it sideways into a channel and lifting it free.

On windows that have sash cords the stop molding will have to be removed first. Insert a broad chisel behind the molding and twist so that the strip comes away only partially at any one point. Work carefully to avoid damaging or breaking the molding. With the strip removed, disen-

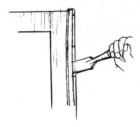

149

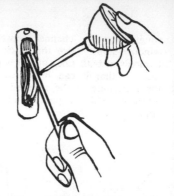

gage the sash cord at both sides. Fasten a nail or strip of wood to the ends of the cords so that they will not slip past the pulley. Lower the weight gently and observe the action of the pulley. If stiff, apply a few drops of oil to the shafts.

If the window has tension strips, try adjusting these first by turning their mounting screws. If this does not work, or if no mechanical adjustment is possible, wood can be sanded or planed from the sides of the sash to make it fit. Do not remove too much material at any one time.

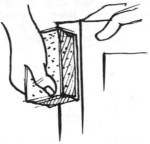

It is a good idea first to clean up and lubricate the channels, then check the fit of window as you plane or sand. It should fit snugly without binding.

When a wood window rattles it is because there is too much space between the sash and its stop molding. An easy way to alleviate this problem is to run a strip of metal or felt weatherstripping into the space. To make a permanent repair, remove the molding and nail it back closer to the sash.

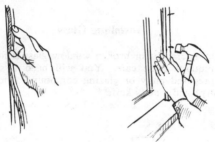

Aluminum casement and sliding windows bind when dirt collects in the tracks. Sometimes the metal becomes pitted, impeding the window's smooth operation. Usually this can be corrected with a cleanup and rubbing with fine steel wool. The tracks should then be lubricated periodically with paraffin or wax. Never try to pry the window with a sharp tool, as this will distort the tracks.

When steel casement windows stick or bind, check to see that hinges are free of rust or accumulated paint. Look for loose hinge screws or for binding in the crank mechanism. Steel wool and lubricating oil will take care of the hinges. It may be necessary to open the handle assembly for cleaning and oiling.

Installing Glass

Replacing cracked or broken window glass is not difficult, but it requires some care. You will need a sharp glass cutter, prepared putty or glazing compound (more flexible than putty) and a putty knife.

Installation of the glass is normally done from the outside, so if you are repairing a second-floor window it may be wise to remove the sash, if that is possible. Use heavy work gloves to remove the broken pieces of glass from the frame. Heat from a soldering gun will help soften the old putty, or a small wood chisel can be used to clean it out, but take care not to damage the frame. Extract the metal glazier's points with pliers.

The replacement glass should be cut ⅟₁₆-inch smaller all around than the frame opening. This is to allow for any irregularities that may exist in the frame.

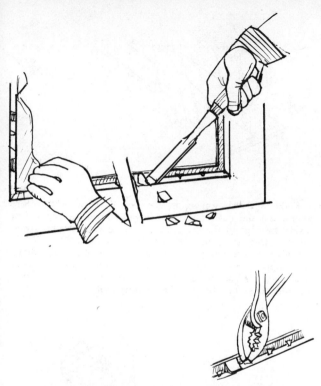

Mark the glass with a sharpened crayon, then turn it over and lay it on a flat surface covered with a thickness of newspaper or an old blanket. A steel straightedge should be used to guide the cut. Any doubts about the glass cutter can be satisfied by first scoring a piece of the old glass: if the score mark shows signs of skipping, the cutting wheel is dull or chipped.

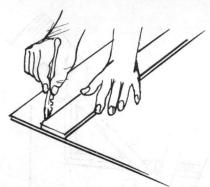

Make sure the glass is free of dust or grit before attempting the cut. The score mark should be begun just inside the edge of the glass farthest from you, then followed through with smooth, even pressure on the cutter. When the glass is scored, you can lay it over the straightedge and apply pressure on both sides of the score to break it cleanly. If the piece to be removed is narrow, snap it off with the slotted head of the cutting tool.

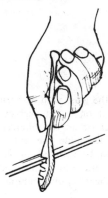

Before the glass can be installed in the frame, the groove should be painted with linseed oil in order to prevent drying out and subsequent cracking of the putty. Apply a ⅛ inch thickness of putty all around the frame. Press the glass into place, making sure it lays flat against the shoulders of the frame. Secure it with the glazier's points, pressing them in 4 to 6 inches apart on all sides.

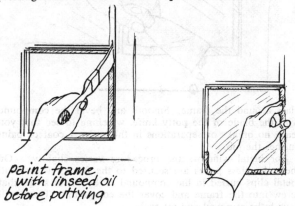

paint frame with linseed oil before putting

Now roll some more putty into a "rope" about ½-inch thick. Use your fingers to press it against the wood and

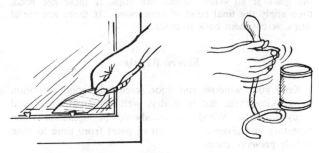

glass around the frame. Smooth and bevel the compound with the blade of the putty knife, watching to see that you leave no breaks or separations in the seal. A coat of paint finishes the job.

For metal windows the procedure varies slightly. On these the glass panes are secured to the frames with small metal clips buried in the compound or by metal strips that screw into the frame and cover the compound. These will have to be removed and set aside.

Lay a bead of glazing compound into the frame and adjust the replacement glass so that the compound meets the glass at all sides. Install the clips, if these are used, then apply the final bead of compound. If there are metal strips, screw them back in place.

Screen Repair

Keep your window and door screens in good condition by stacking them flat in a dry, well-ventilated area until ready for use. Wood frames should be tightened when necessary and given a fresh coat of paint from time to time to help preserve them.

A small hole in screening has a way of mysteriously increasing in size if not patched as soon as it is discovered. If the hole is small enough, a drop or two of waterproof cement will do the job. The cement hardens into a film that covers the hole.

When dealing with larger tears, cut a patch of wire screen material that is wider than the hole by ½ inch. If you do not have extra screen around, patches in various sizes are available at any hardware store.

Unravel two wires at each side of the patch, then bend the end wires at a right angle on all four sides. Place the patch over the hole and thread the bent wires so that they pass evenly to the other side of the screen. They can now be bent back to fix the patch permanently and firmly in position.

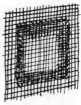

An old or damaged wood screen frame can be renewed easily enough so that you do not have to go to the expense of purchasing a new one. When trouble occurs, it is usually at the frame joints. The joint itself may be loose or the wood broken or rotted.

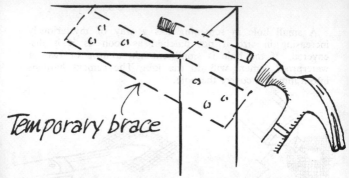

Temporary brace

A joint can be tightened by bracing the frame pieces with a ⅜-inch dowel. Drill a hole through the side member into the top or bottom piece. Coat the dowel with glue and hammer it into the hole, trimming or driving it flush, as the case may be. A damaged section of the frame can be replaced with new wood, which is screwed and cemented into position. If the new piece is at the joint, dowel it as well. When cutting the frame, cut at an angle to mate with the new section.

A sagging screen door can be corrected with the use of a turnbuckle and cable, placed at either side of the door.

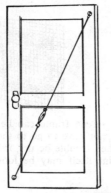

158

Fasten one end of the cable to the top side rail over the hinge; the other end should be screwed to the bottom of the other side rail. Tighten the turnbuckle until the door can swing freely.

To replace screen wire in a wood frame, you must first remove the molding. Use a paint scraper or putty knife for this job, prying gently along the length of the molding until it comes free. Remove all staples or tacks from the frame. Cut the new screen 1-inch wider at all sides with old scissors or metal snips.

You will have to apply tension to the screen when it is tacked to the frame. This is to prevent any stretching later. The best way to do this is to lay the frame across a pair of sawhorses or a work surface as wide as the

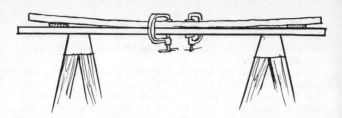

frame. Place a cross board under each end of the frame, then C-clamp the sides of the frame to the work surface so that there is a slight bow formed in the middle.

Tack the new screening tautly at each end, doubling the material where you tack. Now release the C-clamps and tack the screen along the sides of the frame. Replace the molding and trim any wire that sticks out from under it.

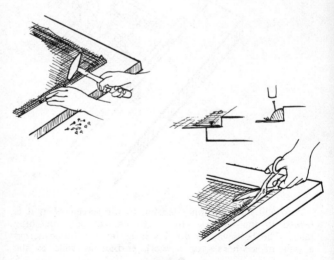

In metal frames, a spline holds the screening in place. This must be pried out to remove the torn screening. New screening is then laid over the framing and trimmed to size, with the corners cut at 45-degree angles. The spline is then tapped back into its groove in the frame to secure the screening.

CHAPTER 9

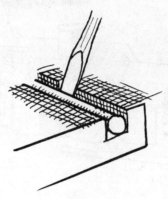

Weatherproofing
and
Insulating

The time to start thinking of ways to improve your home's ability to retain heat is before winter begins. Few home-owners consider the extent of interior heat loss through ill-fitting storm sashes, an uninsulated wall, attic, or floor, and cold-admitting cracks around windows and doors. Added together these heat-wasters can account for a substantial portion of your fuel bills—sometimes as much as 25 percent, the heating specialists say.

Taking steps to see that your house is adequately protected against the weather is not only a sensible precaution for the winter months, but is also a way to insure your comfort in hot weather. Easily installed reflector-type insulation will trap heat inside during the cold spells and also keep heat out when the sun shines brightly. And if your home or any portion of it is artificially airconditioned, the same methods you use to keep cold air from entering will also serve to retain that expensively produced cool air during the summer.

Depending on the materials you select and the construction and condition of your home, most of the work involved in effective weatherproofing can be handled by you cheaply and quickly. The results will be worth it.

Types of Weatherstripping

Used to prevent drafts from entering around windows and doors, weatherstripping is available in a variety of materials, both rigid and flexible. Most common and easiest to apply are the flexible types, which come in roll form. These include the standard felt stripping, metal-backed felt, foam rubber with adhesive backing, vinyl tubular gasket, vinyl-covered sponge, spring bronze or aluminum, and vinyl or metal channel for casement windows.

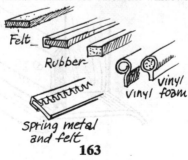

Felt

Rubber

Vinyl
Vinyl foam

Spring metal
and felt

163

The rigid types are made of strips of wood or metal to which are fastened flexible rubber strips or sponge backing. An interlocking rigid metal type is available, but use of this should be left to the professional, since it involves a great deal of preparation for installation.

Generally the flexible types are the best choice for the do-it-yourselfer. Which material you select depends on how much you care to spend and how long you expect the stripping to last. The felt types are the shortest-lived of the lot—two seasons at best. Vinyl stripping is more attractive and wears longer. Adhesive-backed foam rubber does not last a long time, but it may be your only choice for aluminum windows where you wish to avoid nailing. The spring metal stripping is the most expensive, but it also is permanent—and therefore, in the long run, cheapest of them all.

For the bottoms of doors, special rigid weatherstripping is available. The simplest is a metal or aluminum strip with a felt or vinyl sweep that is screwed to the bottom of the door. The sweep presses against the inside of the threshold when the door is closed.

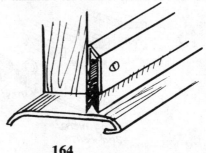

Another type consists of an aluminum channel that fits around the bottom of the door like a sleeve. It has a flexible vinyl facing that presses down over the top of the threshold. Yet another kind replaces the threshold entirely, and has a vinyl inset that provides a seal against the door bottom.

Windows and Doors

Flexible weatherstripping is fast and easy to install. Most types can be cut with scissors; tin snips will be needed for others. Your dealer will recommend the best kind of fastener for the job. With the exception of the spring metal type, all weatherstripping should be fastened so that the flexible, or contact edge presses snugly against a face of the closed window or door. Bend stripping at corners to form a continuous seal, where possible. It should be screwed or nailed every 4 or 5 inches and at every corner where a bend takes place.

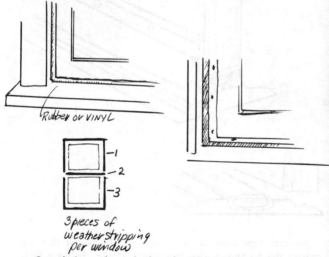

Rubber or VINYL

—1
—2
—3

3 pieces of
weatherstripping
per window

On windows the stripping should be in three pieces, one for each sash and a shorter length to fit where the two sashes meet. Install the sash sections in one continuous strip, nailing the sides to the window stops and the upper and lower sections to the sill and frame. Tack the shorter piece along the top of the lower sash so that it presses against the upper sash. It may be necessary to cut the stripping to fit around the sash lock.

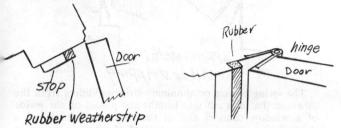

Rubber Weatherstrip

On doors the weatherstripping is fastened in one piece around the door stops. Its placement on the stops depends on the type of stripping used. The felt and foam types are applied to the inside face of the stops. Vinyl tubular stripping should be tacked to the side of the stop so that it presses evenly against the face of the door.

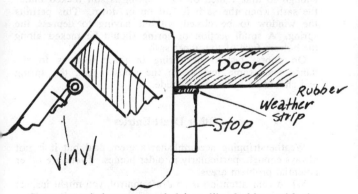

Casement windows are sealed in a like fashion, with the stripping fastened to the stops. Channel stripping of either the metal or vinyl variety should be used for steel windows.

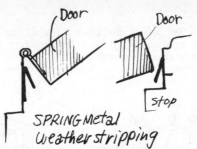

SPRING Metal
weather stripping

The spring bronze or aluminum stripping differs from the others in that it is cut into lengths and placed on the inside of a window channel and at the jambs and frame of a door. It is a two-ply affair, one leaf of which is tacked to the wood while the other presses out against the sides of a window or door to form a draft-resisting seal.

To install on a window, raise the sash up or down, accordingly, and nail the strips to the sash channels with the open leaf facing the outside. Each strip should be long enough so that 1 inch or so of spring is still tucked under the sash when the sash is full up or down. This permits the window to be closed without having to depress the spring. A small section of spring should be tacked along the bottom face of the upper sash.

On doors, fasten the spring in three sections to the jambs and frame just inside the stops; again, the spring leaf should be facing the outside.

Other Draft Entries

Weatherstripping accomplishes a great deal but it is not always enough, particularly in older homes. There are other potential problem areas.

While your attention is on draft control, you might inspect the condition of the putty in all window sashes. If cracked or broken, the putty should be patched or replaced. Check the bottom of the window sills where they meet the wall.

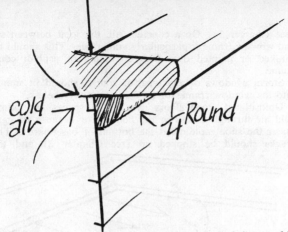

cold air

¼ Round

Settling of the foundation can create a leak point at this spot. Quarter-round molding can be nailed on to cover this.

Outside, check for cracks between the window and the siding and sill, applying caulking compound as necessary

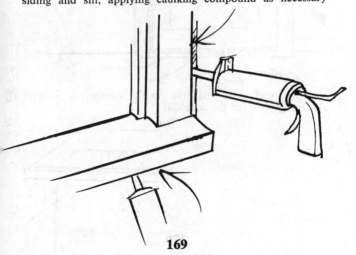

(see Chapter 3). On a concrete sill, the joint between sill and window frame is particularly vulnerable. This should be caulked or painted over with a coating of asphalt compound.

Storm windows of any type, of course, should fit snugly into the window frames or they are virtually useless.

Uninsulated wood floors over crawl spaces can admit cold air through cracks in the flooring or because of gaps under the shoe molding at the bottom of baseboards. The cracks should be stopped up (see Chapter 2) and the

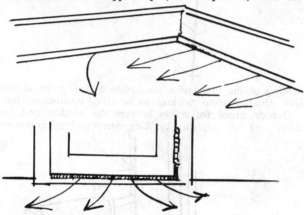

molding pried loose and reset to the baseboard. Inspect also for gaps under the door sills.

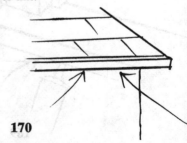

Your winterizing inspection should not omit the outside walls and roofing. Check for loose or broken siding and for cracks or breaks in masonry. Roofs should be inspected and potential leak points repaired. The condition of flashing at roof-to-wall seams and around windows is of particular importance. A review of the respective chapters will assist you in performing these checks and making the necessary repairs. You should then turn your attention to the condition of your home's insulation and the installation of heat-retaining materials where they are needed most.

Use of Insulation

Proper insulation of ceilings and walls is the single most important factor in the climate control of your home. Heat will pass through a wall or roof when there is a difference in temperature on the two sides. The direction of travel is always the same: heat seeks the cold. Thus on a cold day the interior heat will penetrate any material to find its way out, and on a hot day it goes to any lengths to fight its way in. A variety of insulating materials is used to impede this natural process, though none is capable of stopping it completely.

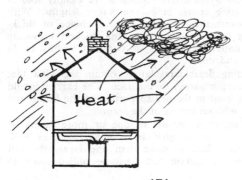

171

Ideally your home was weatherproofed during construction, for only then is it possible to do a truly thorough job. However, if your home is only partially insulated, or the existing insulation is inadequate in key spots, there is still much you can do, or have done, to reduce heat loss and dramatically pare your fuel bills.

Because the roof is the most exposed part of the house, insulation of the attic floor or walls is a must. This kind of work can be handled easily by the homeowner, especially in unfinished areas. Floors over crawl spaces can be weatherproofed effectively. A cold wall especially subject to icy winds, or a wall adjacent to an unheated garage, can be insulated handily without having to call in the contractor.

Insulating materials fall into one of four categories: flexible blankets or batts, loose fill, rigid insulating boards, and reflective foil. The first three function by trapping air within the particular substance, the last reflects radiant heat like a mirror. Which one you use depends largely on the specific application. How much you should use is a matter of the temperature extremes in your part of the country.

Generally, where open joists and studs are to be treated, the flexible insulation in blanket or batt form is the most popular with do-it-yourselfers. Blankets are usually sold in rolls while batting comes in 4- and 8-foot lengths. With this type of weatherproofing you have a choice of thicknesses ranging from 1 to 6 inches, the thickest providing the most insulation. It comes in standard widths to fit between joists and studs.

When selecting flexible insulation, obtain the kind that incorporates a vapor barrier on one face. The barrier should always present itself to the heated portion of the house and should be laid without breaks in the seams.

Reflective insulation consists of one or more layers of aluminum foil. It is effective, but not as much as bulk insulation. When there is more than one layer, the foil is folded accordion-fashion and must be pulled apart to install. It is sometimes difficult to handle because it tears easily. Maximum insulation is gained only when it is installed with air space between it and the surfaces it will protect.

Fill-type insulation comes in bags or bales, usually in loose granular form. It can be made of mineral wool, mica, or wood fiber and is the cheapest of all the materials. For the homeowner, loose fill can be used to insulate the open floors of unoccupied attics. It is simply poured or packed between the joists. It can also be used to fill the space between outside and inside walls.

Rigid panels, ½- to 1-inch thick, come in a wide range of sizes and textures. This finish paneling can be installed over furring strips nailed to walls, with or without batt-type insulation between the old wall and the paneling. By itself, it provides only a small measure of protection, but combined with reflective insulation, it will do an adequate job on a cold wall.

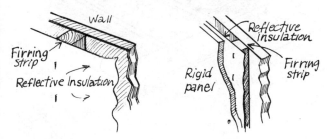

Insulating the Attic

The condition of the attic dictates the means of insulation. If the attic is unfinished, and will remain so, probably the easiest and cheapest method is to insulate the floor with one of the loose fills. Your dealer can estimate the amount you will need if you advise him of the floor area and the degree of protection desired. Manufacturers estimate that heat loss can be reduced by about 12 percent with 1 inch of fill and over 17 percent with 3 inches (more is generally not practicable).

Before fill can be poured, the area between the joists must be covered with a layer of building paper, which is available in rolls. As the end of a roll is reached, overlap the beginning of the next one and tape the joints. Spread the

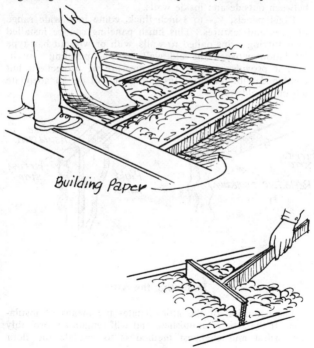

Building Paper

fill as it is poured so that it is consistent in depth at all points. You can make a T-shaped spreader out of heavy cardboard or wood. Lay platforms of planking across the joists to give you firm footing while you work.

In lieu of fill, batt or blanket insulation can be laid between the joists, with the side that has the vapor barrier facing the lower, or heated, portion of the house. The batts should be not less than 3 inches thick, and must lie flat and fill the spaces between the joists exactly. The pockets formed where the joists meet the roof rafters should be filled with clumps of insulation and covered with the same material used for the barrier.

If an attic is heated, or if you plan to finish and heat the area later for living quarters, then the batts or blankets must be installed overhead. Fasten the insulation to the rafters and studs with the vapor barrier side facing into the house. Since the roof requires the greatest amount of insulation, batts should be at least 5 inches thick.

The insulating material is precut to fit between studs of joists, so the only trimming will take place when you come to the end of a space. The batts should be nailed or stapled along each edge to the face of the rafters every 10 to 14 inches, with all seams lapped and secured. On knee

175

Vapor barrier faces inward

Tape ↓

walls, fasten the material to the studs with the vapor barrier facing toward the center of the attic.

Reflective insulation comes in one continuous strip, compressed vertically, in the multiple-layer type, or in rolls with smooth aluminum facing. The single sheeting is applied in much the same manner as batts or blankets. Heavier weights of aluminum should be cut with tin snips or large shears.

When using the accordion-type, begin at the top of the wall or ceiling and staple only one side of it every 6 inches or so until you cover the entire length of the opening. Cut the aluminum at the bottom. With the strip fastened at one side, pull the free side, a little at a time, to the adjoining rafter or stud and staple it there. You must work carefully to avoid tearing the material. If the insulation is faced with a vapor barrier, make sure it points in the right directions—toward the inside of the attic.

Floors and Walls

Floors conduct heat when they are over an unheated basement or crawl space. If the underside of the flooring is accessible, as it would probably be in this situation, you can effectively insulate the floor from underneath.

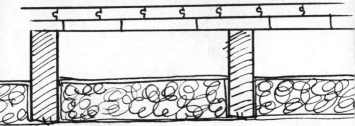

Flexible insulation is best for this job, with a thickness of 2½ to 3 inches providing adequate protection. The batts are nailed to the joists as described above, with the vapor barrier, if any, facing up to the subflooring. Care should be taken to ensure that the seal is complete.

Reflective aluminum can also be used, but it will not insulate to the same degree.

If a floor is finished on both sides, such as may occur over an unheated porch or garage, it is still possible to insulate it by having fill-type material blown into the spaces between the joists.

This same method is used to insulate the walls of a finished house. It is not always satisfactory for walls, because it has a tendency to settle after a time. While both of these jobs should be left to the professional, who has special equipment to force-blow the material into flooring or wall, it is possible for the homeowner to tackle a single wall with insulation of this type.

To do this, holes will have to be cut along the top of the inside wall (the pros work it from the outside) over each space between studs. First pry the crown molding (if any) from the top of the wall. Locate the studs by experimental

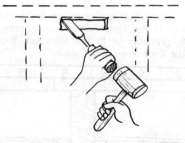

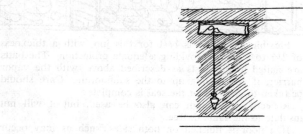

drilling or with a magnetic stud finder and between each pair chisel an opening approximately 8 inches wide by 3 inches deep, breaking through the lathing as well. Tie a plumb bob to a string and drop it down behind the wall to check for cross pieces. If such exist, you will have to locate them and cut an opening below the obstruction. The fill can now be poured through the holes you have made until each cavity is filled with the insulator. Patch the walls (see Chapter 6) and replace molding. All in all, quite a project!

A less tedious proposition is to resurface the old wall with paneling. This is handled by nailing furring strips to the wall and fastening the panels onto that, as described in Chapter 6. The insulating potential of the panels themselves is not great, so batt insulation is fastened between the furring strips. The vapor barrier faces the paneling.

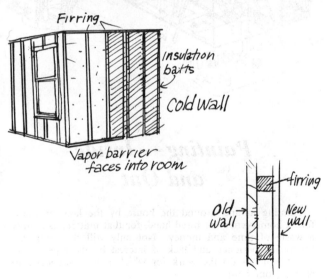

Firring

Insulation batts

Cold wall

Vapor barrier faces into room

firring

Old wall

New wall

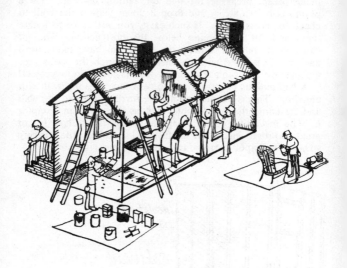

CHAPTER 10

Painting — Inside and Out

Painting in and around the house by the lazy or indifferent homeowner (or hired hand, for that matter) is simply a waste of time and money. Not only will the paint job betray inexperience and lack of interest by its appearance, but it will not do the work for which it was intended: to protect your home.

The key to fine, trouble-free work is in preparation—securing all necessary materials in advance, preparing the surfaces to accept paint, and choosing the right paints for the job at hand.

Many economy-minded amateurs try to take shortcuts in the quality of the materials they purchase. This is a mistake. Cheap tools will make your work more difficult. Bargain paints, some without label "because the price is so low the manufacturer does not want his name known," may not prove to be bargains after all. And stinting in the preparation of surfaces to be painted may result in having to do twice the work.

Painting Tools

Before starting any painting job you must gather together all the tools and materials you need. The reason is simple, though not always obvious: to prevent running out of something vital in the middle of a job, which can sometimes mean starting the entire job over.

Thus you should have on hand, in addition to sufficient paints and brushes, such items as sandpaper, steel wool, patching compounds, scrapers, mixing buckets, plastic drop cloths, masking tape, paint shields, thinners, and solvents.

If you are painting outdoors, strong ladders or rented paint scaffolding are essential.

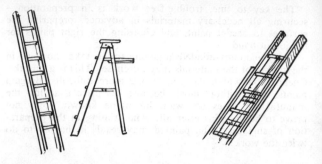

Regardless of which method you use to apply paint, you will need brushes, if only to cover those areas inaccessible to roller or spray gun. Use the widest brush practicable: on walls, for example, a good size is 4 to 6 inches; paneling, woodwork, and trim, from 1 to 3 inches; and for sashes, a minimum of 1 inch. The idea is to use the fewest strokes possible to cover the surface; it will save time and result in a neater job.

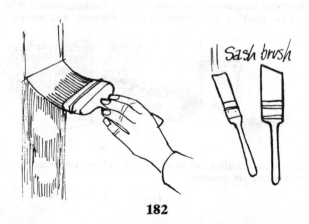

Sash brush

For many years, hog bristle was considered the only "quality" material for a brush. The new nylon bristles with exploded tips perform just as well, or better. The higher the percentage of exploded, or "flagged," tips a brush has, the better it will apply paint. Moreover, a good brush will be thicker at the ferrule, indicating more paint-holding bristles (but check to see that the brush does not just have a thick filler block in its center to give it a thicker appearance).

Press the brush against a firm surface. It should feel springy and the bristles should not "fan" excessively. For painting pipes and railings, a round or oval brush is best. A chisel-tipped brush is recommended for use with enamels.

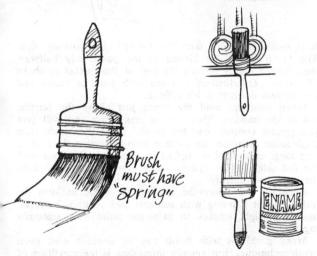

Brush must have "spring"

Good brushwork will assure a quality paint job and avoid difficulties later. Always attempt to wield the brush with the bristles pointed slightly downward. This keeps paint from building up at the ferrules and dripping over your work.

It is easiest to paint with the bucket only partially full. The brush should be dipped in the paint only halfway, then tapped lightly against the rim of the bucket to shake off excess. Overloading a brush with paint is messy and will make a uniform finish difficult.

When painting, hold the brush just above the ferrule, not at the handle. This will be less tiring and will give you greater control over the brush. Load the brush, then daub some paint on the surface before starting the stroke. Use long, even strokes applied in alternate directions with the flat sides of the brush. Once you develop a rhythm, the work goes quickly.

Generally the fewer the strokes, the more uniform the finish. When painting with enamels and varnish, however, use short, light strokes to help the paint flow smoothly together.

Many problems with finish can be avoided with good brush technique. But equally important is the condition of the brushes. A brush will hold more paint and ensure smoother application if it is clean and flexible, with all loose bristles removed by hand. You can precondition a brush by soaking it in linseed oil the night before use.

Brushes should be cleaned immediately after they are used and stored to protect them for further successful use. Begin by "painting" sheets of newspaper until you have worked out most of the remaining paint. If a water-base paint was used, simply wash the brush under running water.

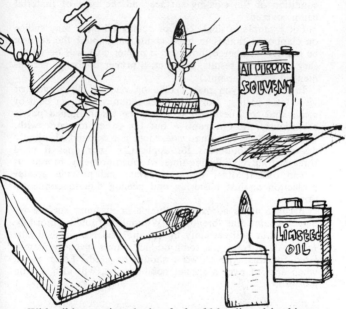

With oil-base paints the brush should be dipped in thinner or solvent for several minutes. Knead the bristles in the solvent until all paint is loose, dipping the brush in fresh solvent as often as necessary to remove all traces. Then wash the brush with soap and water, rinse thoroughly, and wrap the bristles in heavy paper or foil. If the brush is to be stored for a long period, first soak it in linseed oil.

Oil paints generally require the least preparation since they have strong penetrating and adhesive properties. Paints in the acrylic or vinyl latex group demand more attention in preparing the surface, but they have other qualities that recommend them. Generally your choice is governed by the condition of the existing surface and the type of material being covered.

For example, a single coat of quality oil paint may suffice on clapboard that is in good condition. Should the surface be heavily weathered, however, a primer coat will be necessary. (For best results, however, a primer is always recommended with oil paint.)

In this case you may decide on one of the acrylic or vinyl latex paints. Normally latex requires a primer coat of some kind for successful service. The water-thinned paints are slightly more expensive but far easier to work with. Unlike oil-base coverings, latex does not demand absolutely dry weather conditions for application—nor does it need three or four days' drying time. Applied properly, moreover, it can outlast other types of paints and provide greater protection against blistering and peeling due to condensation.

Because of its porosity, a shingle or masonry surface requires a paint that "breathes." Without this quality, moisture from within will certainly blister and peel the finished surface. Alkyd resin and some oil-base paints specially formulated for this type of work should be used. Latex paint, when applied over a special bonding coat, will also do the job well.

For masonry there is also an inexpensive Portland cement paint, which is a mixture of Portland cement and alkali-resistant pigment with a water base. This type can be applied only over unpainted masonry or masonry that has been previously painted with the same material.

Since the pigments in paint settle to the bottom, any paint must be mixed thoroughly before use or it will not flow smoothly and consistently. Ideally your dealer will perform this service with a mechanical agitator (not recommended for latex) which mixes the paint without your having to open the container.

The technique of mixing by hand is called "boxing," and it is as effective as mechanical agitation if you are thorough. First remove the lid from the paint container and pour off the thin liquid into a clean receptacle. With a paint paddle stir the collected pigment to a creamy consistency. Slowly add the thin liquid, stirring all the time. When this has been mixed, pour the entire quantity into the second container and mix some more, then repeat this step two or three times.

Remember also to stir the paint occasionally while you are painting.

Rollers and Spray Guns

Rollers are popular because they can cover large areas in a very short time. What's more, the roller can be used to good result with almost any type of paint on the market (enamels and shellac are exceptions) and on any surface, including rough-textured walls such as stucco and brick. With an extension handle added, the roller is a boon for working on ceilings and high walls.

Several types of rollers are available, but the most popular and easiest to use is the dip or tray type that has a replaceable cover.

Buy only top quality roller covers, since the end result of your painting will be influenced largely by how well the synthetic fiber absorbs and releases the paint. Covers are available in naps of varying thickness, anywhere from ⅜-inch to 1½-inches, the thickest for use on rough surfaces. The nap most used for ceilings and walls with either water or oil paints is between ⅜- and ½-inch thick. As with brushes, choose the widest roller you can handle comfortably. Small rollers are available for painting corners.

A special paint pan, or tray, is used to feed the roller. It must be as wide as the widest roller you are using, and capable of being fastened securely to a stepladder for high work. When painting surfaces from ground level, it will be easier on your back if the pan is elevated on a firm base of some kind.

Only the lower, sloping portion of the pan is filled with paint. The roller is then dipped into the paint and run back and forth lightly across the ridged upper portion of the tray to remove the excess. Always begin rolling on an upstroke, if you are painting a wall, or away from you when covering a ceiling. This is to prevent splatter on you and on the work. Stroke smoothly and without hurry, so that the roller does not spin. Lap each stroke by one-half its width and crisscross the strokes lightly to avoid missing spots—easy to do

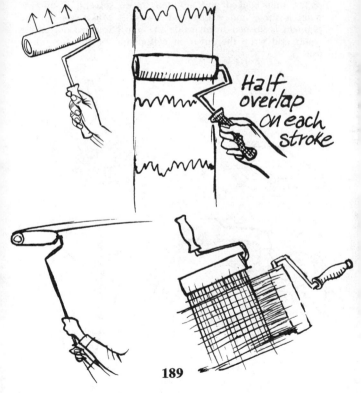

Half overlap on each stroke

if there is little contrast between new paint and the old surface. Paint all corners first, using a brush or corner roller, then proceed to fill in the large areas.

Many homeowners who do their own roller painting simply throw the roller away after use. This is self-defeating, particularly when the reason you are painting is to save money. The cleanup job can be eased some by lining the bottom of the paint pan with tin foil. After use, the roller should be passed back and forth over old newspaper, then soaked and agitated under solvent, if oil-base paint is used, and wrung and washed. Make sure all the pigment is flushed from inside the nap. Squeeze out excess water and wrap the cover in cellophane or foil for future use.

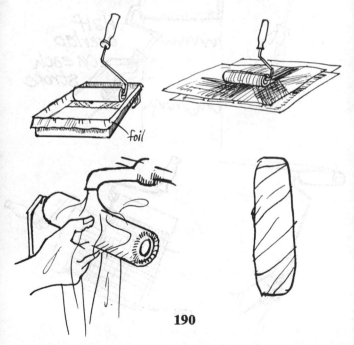

Spray guns are ideal for painting open work surfaces such as lattices and fences of any kind. In the proper hands, they can apply an outstanding, nearly faultless finish to inside and outside walls. But note the qualifier. Use of a spray gun on large surfaces demands a high-quality, heavy-duty unit and the skill required to use it.

However, there are a number of light-duty sprayers available for sale or rent that can be used successfully around the home. If the job is small and you are not too choosy about colors, there are also aerosol spray cans.

The biggest problem experienced with any spray gun is the clogging of tip and filter passages with accumulated paint or foreign matter. Be sure to follow the cleaning and clearing recommendations for the particular unit you obtain.

Spraying should always be done in a well-ventilated room. Since the spray carries far, make sure surrounding surfaces are well protected. Obtain a respirator or fashion a mask from fabric to prevent breathing in the spray.

The technique in spraying is always to move the gun parallel to the surface being painted. Never spray in an arc.

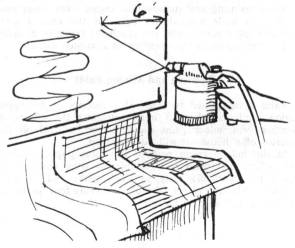

The gun should be held at a uniform 6 to 9 inches from the work area, stroking back and forth horizontally and lapping each stroke by about 50 percent.

Always keep the gun moving to avoid the build-up of paint, and keep the trigger fully depressed until an entire area has been covered, if this is possible in one go. The trick here is to begin before the edge of a flat surface and end past the opposite edge. This will ensure an even application of spray (providing the spray has been kept equidistant for the entire stroke).

When painting any surface that angles away from you, such as a table top, always begin at the edge nearest you and spray across until you reach the far edge in order to prevent overspray from settling on a painted surface.

Choosing and Mixing Paint

Paint is designated for use either indoors or for application outdoors where it must withstand the effects of weather. An indoor paint should never be used on the exterior of a house—it will not stand up.

In the indoor group perhaps the most popular choice for ceilings and walls is water-thinned latex paint. It is fast-drying, washable, easy to work with, and virtually odorless. Flat oil paints take about twenty-four hours to dry (versus half an hour for latex).

Semigloss oil and alkyd resin paints wear well and have high moisture-resistant properties, and thus are good choices for kitchen and bath, and for trim around doors and windows. Wall enamels are used for these same areas and provide the toughest covering possible. But note that a primer coat will be necessary to obtain a first-rate enamel finish.

Exterior paints fall into three categories, all available in oil or latex bases: "trim" paints for use around doors, windows, and shutters; "floor and deck" paints that have special scuff- and wear-resistant qualities; and "house" paints for covering of siding.

A good exterior paint job should last about five years, providing the surface has been prepared and existing paint or surface problems corrected (see "Exterior Painting"). Because of the work and expense involved, you must consider carefully the type of paint you will use. It is a good idea to discuss the matter thoroughly with a dealer who is knowledgeable on the subject.

Exterior Painting

No paint can be expected to bond effectively to a surface that is loose, scaling, powdery, or greasy. If the existing paint job exhibits signs of unusual wear or decay, just covering it with paint will be a waste of time; the new coat will inherit the problem (see "Paint Problems and Cures").

To prepare the surface for painting, carefully inspect the exterior of the house for loose, warped, or cracked boards and make any necessary repairs (see Chapter 3). Replace and set all loose nails and prime exposed nailheads to prevent rust. Fill depressions in the siding with putty and sand level.

Pay particular attention to joints between siding and window and door frames. Any openings here can admit paint-damaging moisture. Seal such cracks with caulking compound. Likewise, check the condition of flashing, gutters, and downspouts and caulk or putty where necessary.

If you will be painting over a glossy surface, the old paint must first be sanded to give it "tooth." A disc-sander is the fastest tool for this job.

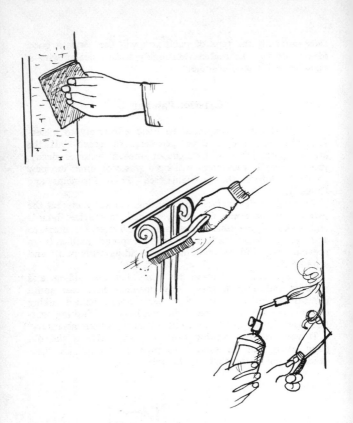

Smooth all rough spots on the siding with a coarse sandpaper block. A stiff wire brush is ideal for removing dirt, paint scale, and other loose material that may affect the paint job. If several layers of damaged paint must be removed, soften the old paint with a blowtorch or one of the combination electric softener-scrapers on the market.

Exercise extreme caution when using a blowtorch, applying just enough heat to loosen the paint for scraping. An alternative method is to coat the area with a chemical paint remover. This works especially well on windows that have many layers of accumulated paint.

When old paint is removed to the bare wood, the area should be given one or more coats of primer. Feather the surrounding edges to permit a smooth finish.

It is always a good idea to give the outside of the house a good washing before any painting is attempted. Some-

times water under pressure is enough to remove dirt and light chalking. If dirt buildup is severe, however, a detergent and some scrubbing may be necessary.

Masonry surfaces scheduled for painting should be washed to remove dirt and dust. Oil and grease stains and efflorescence should be treated with appropriate solvents. All cracks and open joints should be filled with patching compound.

When painting the house, begin at the top and work your way down. (See "Ladders and Scaffolding," Chapter 5.) Leave windows for last and remove shutters for painting at your leisure. Protect the ground around the house with drop cloths.

Weather is an important factor. Avoid painting in temperatures below 50 or higher than 90 degrees, and try to arrange your painting schedule so that you do not have occasion to paint a side when it is exposed to direct intense sunlight. Latex paints can be applied over damp surfaces, but oil paint must be applied to an absolutely dry surface or the paint will not adhere. Wait for a dry spell, or at least three days after rain, before painting.

Exterior Paint Problems and Cures

Excessive chalking. All paints chalk to some degree. It is part of the normal wear process. When chalk dust is

198

abundant, however, it is a sign of failure in the paint. Often the trouble is due either to paint that was thinned too much when applied or to paint of inferior quality. Wash the surface with a stiff brush and water, and give it two coats of paint. If latex is used, the primer coat should contain a special bonding agent.

Blistering and peeling are the result of moisture penetration. They may be due to dampness entering the walls through open siding or open joints around windows and doors, and at the roof line. Or condensation from within the house may be penetrating to the outside walls. Whatever the source of leakage, it must be corrected before applying new paint (see Chapter 3). Two coats of an alkyd resin or latex paint will offer good protection.

Checking normally occurs when a finish is applied over a priming coat that was not permitted to dry thoroughly. Light cracks form on the hard outside coating because the inside coat was soft and moved. The trouble is not serious and can usually be corrected by sanding and applying two coats of paint, allowing sufficient drying time between coats.

Alligatoring consists of hidelike interlacing lines that have formed over the paint film, exposing the layers of paint below. It is usually the result of incompatible coats of

paint, but may also be due to having painted over a greasy or oily surface. Unlike checking, an alligatored surface must be removed to the bare wood before painting is begun.

Bleeding takes the form of gumminess and discoloration in the paint. It can be caused by the action of solvent in the paint or, more often, by the presence of resins and sap in unseasoned wood. Painting over creosoted surfaces may also be a cause. The affected area must be sanded down to the bare wood and a sealer applied before painting.

Crawling is a condition observed soon after paint is applied, and is characterized by drops and globules that form in the new covering. The fault may be due to having

applied a glossy coat over another glossy coat that was not prepared by sanding, by having painted over a greasy surface, or by having applied paint on a cold day.

Mildew is a paint-discoloring fungus common in warm, humid climates and in parts of the house always shaded by plants or shrubs. Even if painted over, the fungus will continue to grow, so it must first be removed. Treat such areas with a solution of trisodium phosphate and water, rinsing well, then applying a fungus-resistant paint after the wall is thoroughly dry.

Interior Painting

Before starting to paint walls, ceilings, and woodwork in a room, a certain amount of preparation is necessary. The job will be made easier if all or most of the furniture is removed from the room rather than piled in the center. Floors and any remaining furniture pieces can be protected with drop cloths.

The usual sequence in painting is to do the ceiling first, then the walls, and finally the doors and windows. If surfaces are in good condition and not too grimy, a simple vacuuming or wipe with a damp cloth will be preparation enough. Otherwise a good scrubbing with detergent is necessary.

The painting job will be made simpler if you remove all switch and socket plates from the walls. If it does not entail a great deal of work, remove ceiling light fixtures also. When this is too difficult use masking tape to protect the base of the fixture.

All holes, cracks, or breaks in plaster or wallboard should be patched with spackling compound, sanded, and primed with a primer coat. If the existing paint is glossy, dull it with sandpaper, steel wool, or one of the liquid preparations sold for this purpose. Nail down, reset, or replace all loose, warped, or broken molding.

Loose and scaling paint should be scraped off and the surface sanded and primed with a primer coat. If a plaster wall is particularly rough-textured, you can go over the surface with an electric sander. Fill remaining depressions with spackle, then sand, and give the wall a primer coat.

Wallpaper can be safely painted over if it is well adhered and free of blisters. Trouble, if any, occurs if the pattern on the paper is so prominent that it takes several coats to hide it, or when its dyes are not fast. It is best to paint a test patch before doing the entire wall.

Any loose seams in the paper should be pasted back in place. If the seams are of the overlap type they should be

sanded smooth. Should it be necessary to scrape off a large section of wallpaper, cement a piece of scrap wallpaper in its place to make the wall surface even.

Removing the wallpaper entirely is tedious work, but if its condition is bad you must do it to ensure a proper paint job. A wallpaper steamer can be hired to make the work a lot easier. Never paint over two layers of wallpaper, no matter how secure the paper may seem. The weight of the paint may pull it off in spots.

Painting windows and paneled doors can be much simplified if you follow the correct sequence. On a double-hung window, raise the bottom sash as far as it will go and lower the top sash at least half way. Paint the exposed part of the top sash, then reverse the position of the two sashes so that the remainder of the top one can be painted.

Leave the sashes open a few inches at the top and bottom. Now paint the bottom sash, then go on to the exposed sash channels, top and bottom. Paint all frame and stop molding edges first, leaving the faces and sill for last. Leave the window partly open until the paint dries.

To avoid smearing paint on the glass, mask the edges of the panes with tape or use a paint shield while you work. A sash brush with a chiseled tip will make the work go faster.

On a paneled door, remove as much of the door hardware as possible. Paint the casing first and the edge of the door next. Paint the edges of the molding around inset panels, then the panels themselves. Now paint the horizontal panel separations, and finish by painting the door stiles.

CHAPTER 11

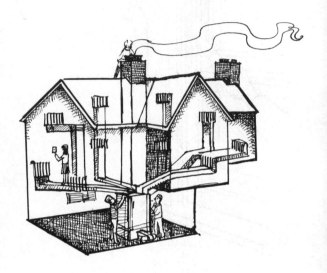

Heating, Cooling, and Ventilating

Many homeowners take for granted the carefree functioning of their home's heating system. Until it goes awry, that is. Then there are frantic calls to the repairman.

While there is no substitute for periodic servicing by a heating specialist, there is much you can do to help prevent breakdowns and to increase heating efficiency. And when problems arise you should know what and where to check before picking up the phone—it can save you time and money.

Similarly, in the cooling of your home during the summer months you can take simple steps to help air-conditioners operate at peak efficiency. Or it may be possible to increase a window unit's cooling potential by placing it in a key part of the house.

Even without mechanical cooling systems your hot-weather comfort can be improved considerably through the correct use of ventilating fans, insulation, or awnings. Often the mere installation of an attic fan can produce remarkable results throughout the entire house.

Central Heating Systems

A heating system is a balanced mechanism that depends on the proper functioning of all components to deliver heat efficiently. The most common oil- or gas-fueled systems—hot water, steam, and forced warm air—require periodic inspection and adjustment before and during the heating season.

In a *hot-water system,* water is heated in a boiler and pumped under pressure via pipes to the rooms of the house. The pump brings cooled water from the room radiators back to the boiler for reheating, then forces this heated water back through the house. The house thermostat turns on the boiler and circulating pump when the temperature falls below a preset figure. Another sensing switch turns off the boiler independently of the pump when water temperature goes beyond a safe level.

The most important thing to remember with this type of system is that there must always be water in the heating circuit—boiler, pipes, and radiator or convector outlets. If

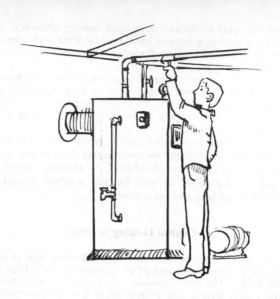

air pockets exist at any point, the heating function in that section of the house will be impaired. Most boilers are equipped with a gauge that indicates water pressure and altitude. The gauge has two indicators, one fixed and showing the recommended level, the other showing the actual pressure. Modern systems incorporate a pressure-reducing valve that automatically feeds water into the boiler when pressure drops. But if this fails, the job must be done manually with a feed valve provided for that purpose. The gauge should be checked at least fortnightly during the heating season and water added to maintain the correct pressure. Never add water when the boiler is hot.

Radiators in hot-water systems are equipped with a bleed valve to permit the release of trapped air. Each radiator should be bled of air periodically.

With a *steam-heat system* only the boiler contains water. When the thermostat actuates the system, the boiler water is heated and converted to steam, which is then sent by its own pressure through pipes to radiator outlets in the home. As the steam cools in the radiators it is condensed and returns to the boiler as water.

Most systems use a single pipe link between boiler and room outlets; others have two pipes at the radiator, one for steam and the other to return the water.

A pressure-relief valve on the boiler releases steam when pressure in the system rises beyond a preset figure. If the valve releases steam continuously, it is a sign of wear. The unit should be replaced.

Water must be kept at a certain level in the boiler. Newer systems have automatic controls to feed water as it is

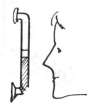

needed, first shutting down the burner. This level can be observed in a tubular glass water gauge at the side of the boiler. The water should be at the halfway point, if not otherwise marked. If you add water manually make sure to first shut down the burner and let the boiler cool somewhat. Add just enough, a little at a time, to bring the water to the correct level.

Radiators using this type of system are equipped with an air valve that automatically releases air so the steam can enter, and a manual shutoff valve. If the air valve is clogged or worn, the unit should be shut down and the valve removed for cleaning or replacement.

A *forced-warm-air system* depends on a network of ducts to deliver warmed air through registers in the walls or floors of the house. As the warm air pushes into the rooms, it drives the heavier cold air through return registers to the furnace for heating.

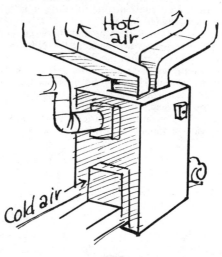

The house thermostat turns on the gas or oil burner to heat air around the system's combustion chamber. When the air in the chamber reaches the correct temperature (around 180 degrees) the blower turns on automatically to deliver the warmed air to the rooms. The return air passes through a filter that should be replaced or cleaned at regular intervals. If the filter is clogged it will impair the efficiency of the entire system.

Some warm-air units can be cycled to operate for longer intervals or even continuously in bitter-cold weather. This arrangement has proved generally more efficient and economical than having the system work intensively then shut down until the temperature drops once again.

The idea is to avoid the long warmup period required to heat the air around the combustion chamber and to prevent cold blasts of air from the registers as the system first delivers after a shutdown. You may decide to have your system adjusted to this type of cycling. If it is already cycled this way the thermostat and furnace settings should be checked regularly by a heating serviceman.

Radiant heating systems that use concealed hot-water tubing or electrical cable to deliver heat through slab floors usually require very little attention on your part, other than periodic servicing of the hot-water boiler and circulator, if such are used.

Routine Maintenance

A good many heating problems can be avoided if you inspect and service the following components of your system in the course of the season and just before cold weather sets in.

Motors, blowers, and fans should be kept free of grease and dirt. Oil-burner motors, circulating motors and pumps, and blowers and blower motors should be lubricated two or three times a year. Apply a few drops of No.-10-weight

oil (unless another weight is specified) to bearings. Wipe fan blades clean and check the condition of the fan belt, replacing or tightening as required. The belt should have a certain amount of slack, but be tight enough to prevent slippage.

Boilers must be checked for proper water level during the season, and should be drained partially or fully at least once a year to remove sediment and rust. First shut the system down to permit the boiler to cool. Turn off the cold water feed valve to the boiler. Attach a garden hose to

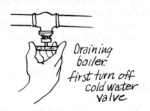

Draining boiler. first turn off cold water valve

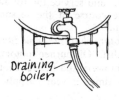

Draining boiler

the drain cock at the bottom of the boiler and open the cock to drain water. A bucket will do if you are removing small quantities of rust-laden water. To flush the entire system, permit all water to drain out, then open the feed valve. When clean water comes out of the hose, close the drain cock and continue adding fresh water to the required level.

Hot-water systems equipped with overhead *expansion tanks* in which a certain level of air pressure is maintained while the system operates. To drain dirty water from this unit and the pipes, shut the valve between boiler and tank and open the tank's drain cock. A bucket or hose can be used to catch or direct the water. Permit it to drain fully, then seal it and reopen the valve connecting it to the system. Add water slowly until the two arrows on the water altitude gauge line up. Vent the radiators of air, then recheck the water gauge periodically.

Radiators and convectors should be wiped or vacuumed at the start of the season and kept clean. Hot-water units have air vents that should be opened when the system is first started to release trapped air. Start at the top of the

house and work your way down, opening each vent until water spurts out. If a radiator does not heat adequately, trapped air is the probable cause—assuming the shutoff valve is opened.

On steam radiators, the vent valves are fixed to release

air automatically, and if plugged they will prevent steam from filling the radiator. You can sometimes unplug a valve by boiling it in water for twenty minutes or so. Check also that radiators are level on the floor. If not, condensed water will not drain properly, reducing heat output and often resulting in noises in the system. Wood leveling blocks can be slipped under the legs of the radiator to remedy this. (A partially open shutoff valve can also produce hammering and knocking noises.)

If a leak exists at a radiator shutoff valve, first try tightening the packing nut. If this fails, shut the valve, allow it to cool, then loosen and slide the packing nut up on the shaft. Wind valve packing, available at any hardware store, around the shaft under the nut, then retighten. On hot-water radiators the system must first be drained to a level below the defective radiator before this repair can be attempted.

Filters and registers in forced-air systems should be cleaned at the start of the season. Remove wall or floor registers and run a vacuum cleaner hose down into the ducts. It is also a good idea to vacuum around and inside the blower section of the heater (with power turned off). The air filter should be checked several times during the season. Some filters can be cleaned simply by knocking off accumulated dust, others must be replaced when dirty. If the latter kind, keep several on hand.

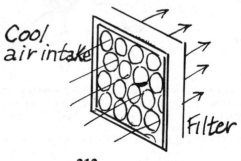

Oil burners should be checked by a heating man each year before the system goes into operation. Usually your utility or fuel supplier will provide this service, and your own contribution is limited to keeping the unit clean and oiled. If the unit burns faintly or with a great deal of smoke, check the air intake in the housing. While the furance is burning adjust the intake until the flame burns brightly and without smoke. A weak flame may also indicate that not enough oil is being fed to the burner, even though the tank is full.

First check the oil-flow adjustment screw on the pump housing—this is located opposite the oil intake—and turn it until the flame burns brightly. If this has no effect, the trouble may be that the pump's oil filter is clogged. This

can be inspected by first shutting off the burner, then removing the pump cap to get at the filter. Wash the filter in clean oil or kerosene.

Chimneys and stovepipes should be checked for leaks at the start of the season. Inspect all joints in the metal

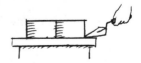

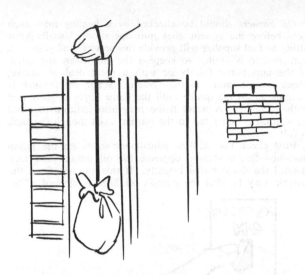

or asbestos-cement stovepipe between the boiler and the chimney. Pay close attention to the pipe where it joins the chimney. If loose, seal the joint with asbestos cement or mortar. Chimneys that pass oil exhaust should be cleaned periodically to avoid the possibility of fire from soot deposits. A simple way to do this is with a weighted burlap bag that is stuffed with shredded newspaper or rags to give it bulk. Tie the end of the bag to a strong cord and lower it from the roof down the chimney, working it up and down to loosen soot on the flue walls. The accumulations can be removed through the trap at the base of the chimney.

Shutting Down for the Season

Your heating system will respond better next time around if you take the relatively little time and effort required properly to shut down the equipment for the summer. Grease, dirt, and rust are the worst enemies of the system, thus all components should be cleaned and oiled. This is also an excellent time thoroughly to flush boilers to remove rust and scale deposits. A rust-inhibiting agent can be introduced along with clean water.

Rather than emptied, however, the systems should be kept completely filled with water throughout the summer. This is to prevent condensation from creating more rust. Enough water should be added to the entire system of a hot-water boiler so that the expansion tank is partly filled. It is a good idea also to fire the system long enough to bring it up to operating temperature, bleed the radiators, then shut down for the summer's duration.

On a steam system, which normally requires only partial filling, the boiler should be filled completely with water and left that way for the summer, after all radiator valves are shut off. (You must remember to bring the water level back down to normal before starting up again the following winter.)

Because condensation will form in a partly empty oil storage tank, it is good practice to keep the tank full even when not being used. Water will settle to the bottom of the tank where it will rust the metal and create pinhole leaks in the tank. You can combat this in buried tanks by introducing a sealer and inhibitor made for this purpose. On indoor storage units, pinhole leaks can be stopped effectively with sealing compounds applied over the holes. The tank should be given a protective coat of paint.

Heating Problem Checklist

When heating problems arise in your system there are points you should check before calling the repairman. It can save you money and perhaps avoid long, cold shutdowns between your call(s) and his arrival.

Failure to Start

1. Check thermostat. Jiggle level or dial to make sure a particle of dirt is not preventing contact.

2. Make sure burner emergency switch has not accidentally been turned off.

3. Check for blown fuse in heating system electrical circuit. Replace if necessary.
4. Check oil-storage tank with dipstick—oil gauge may be defective.
5. Check overload switch on oil burner motor, usually a red button that pops up when motor is overheated. If motor again turns off when button is depressed, do not persist—call the repairman.

6. Check for free operation of stack switch on burner stovepipe—a safety device that automatically turns off burner motor when fuel fails to ignite. Call repairman if motor turns off after starting.
7. Check water level of boilers. Most units are equipped with low-level cutouts. Add water slowly to cooled system.

Insufficient Heat

1. Check thermostat setting. Make sure heat from a nearby electric appliance is not giving the sensor a false impression.
2. Inspect level of water in boiler. On hot water unit, check that expansion tank is not overfull (it should

be only half full). Cut off supply to tank and partially drain tank.

3. Check for trapped air in system, bleeding radiators as required.
4. On steam boilers check for loss of pressure through defective safety valve. Shut down system and replace valve.
5. On hot air units, check to see if air filter is clogged. Clean or replace. Look for loose or broken blower fan belt and adjust or replace.

Cooling and Ventilating

You do not need central air-conditioning to survive a long, hot summer. Comfort inside the home can be improved considerably through the use of exhaust fans and an understanding of climate control methods. The chief thing to keep in mind is that moving air is a good deal more comfortable than stagnant air, and that air pulled from a shaded part of the house is cooler than that found on a sunny side.

In the summer, temperatures in an attic can climb well over 100 degrees. Since heat seeks the cooler air, this

heat is transmitted through the floors and ceilings to affect all levels of the home. Proper insulation of the attic walls and ceilings will help resist heat absorption from the roof. If your attic is presently uninsulated, or if you live in a milder clime and believe insulation is not needed for cold weather protection, you should at least consider installing one of the thin reflective aluminum insulating materials available (see Chapter 9, "Weatherproofing and Insulating").

Exhaust fans placed at key locations—kitchen, bathroom, laundry room, and attic—will help remove hot air and also

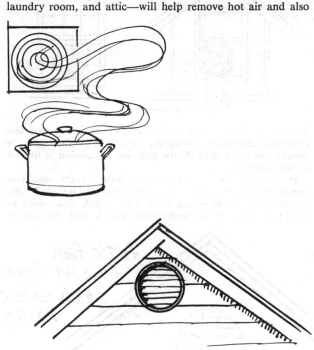

combat excessive humidity in the home. The simplest arrangement is to use window fans at these locations. A more satisfactory alternative is to install them as wall units vented to the outside via adjustable louvers, which can be shut when not needed.

Intake-exhaust window fans can be used to circulate cooled air through the house. They should be arranged so

that air is drawn from a shaded part of the house and exhausted elsewhere. However, since fans of this type are usually not too powerful, the effective circulation is limited to only a small area.

In many homes—especially one-floor layouts—the best ventilation setup possible is a permanently installed attic fan that can be activated by a wall switch downstairs or automatically with a combination switch and thermostat.

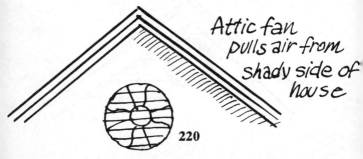

Attic fan pulls air from shady side of house

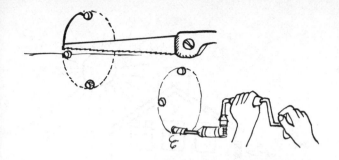

You can have such units installed or tackle the installation yourself, following directions provided with the unit. In addition to lowering temperatures, the fan will provide a steady flow of fresh air through the house.

To be effective the fan must be of a size scaled to your house. It can be mounted centrally in the attic or anywhere on the attic walls, and it must exhaust to the outside of the house. In addition, vents (or a vent, depending on the layout of the house) must be installed within the home to permit the free flow of air drawn by the fan.

Window air conditioners are available today at fairly reasonable cost. (Make certain your electrical wiring will support it!) Sometimes one or two of these units can cool a small house if cooled air is helped along with a fan. Naturally all windows and doors must be kept shut.

Like any other piece of equipment, air conditioners need regular servicing to maintain their efficiency. Filters can clog and impair operation. Depending upon the type of unit, you should clean or replace the filter at the start of the season. If the air conditioner is used extensively, replace the filter midseason as well. It is good practice to locate the air conditioner on a side of the house that gets the most shade. If this is impractical, a window awning should be installed to put the unit in shade.

Central air-conditioning equipment requires periodic cleaning, oiling of fan motors, and cleaning or replacement

221

Airconditioners placed on shady side of house

of filters. It is a good policy to have this done once a year, just as with a furnace, under a service contract. (Filters may have to be checked more frequently, depending on the volume of solid particles that are removed from the air in the area in which you live.) When something goes wrong with the system, it is best to call a professional serviceman, even if it means you may have to swelter for a couple of hours or longer. A central air-conditioning unit is too complex a piece of machinery for the untrained amateur to attempt to repair.

Lowering Fuel Bills

Here are two tips that can result in dramatic fuel savings in the course of a year.

• Thermostat: Adjust it to a comfortable setting for the household—and leave it there! Jiggling it on and off during the day wastes fuel. Added up over a season, the cost to you can be high. You can also save fuel by lowering the thermostat a few degrees before you retire at night. But do not lower it too much or the system will have to pump that much harder in the morning.

• Fuel Flow: Oil burner nozzles should be replaced once a year. The passage of oil at high pressure will widen the passages in the nozzle and result in the use of more fuel than is needed. It will also cause smoking. Experts say savings by taking this precaution can amount to fifty dollars or more per year. If your serviceman is not replacing this inexpensive item, demand that he do so.

CHAPTER **12**

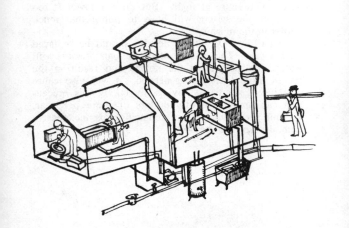

The Plumbing System

If you called the plumber every time something went wrong with your home's plumbing system, your household maintenance expenses would rocket sky-high. Yet, amazingly enough, many homeowners do just that—where a simple do-it-yourself repair might serve instead.

Many of the often-encountered problems with home plumbing can be handled with little fuss and at small expense. Stopped sinks and toilets, leaky faucets and balky toilet flush mechanisms fall into this category. Often a minor adjustment or replacement of some small part is all that is needed. You can avoid high labor bills by doing the job yourself.

You should also be prepared to handle other problems in the plumbing system in case of emergency, and familiarize yourself with the location of main shutoff valves that control the supply of water to the house. Pipes blocked by frozen water can be cleared safely if you know how. Condensation on pipes can be eliminated easily with inexpensive insulation materials. Leaks in pipes can often be fixed without need for pipe replacement.

Clogged Drains

A home's drainage system works on the principle of gravity (unlike the fresh water supply, which operates on pressure). Drains in sinks, bathtubs, and toilets all empty into pipes of increasing diameter that ultimately lead to the main public sewerage line, or, in rural and some suburban communities, to the cesspool or septic tank.

When utility drains back up it is usually because the trap under the drain has become blocked. This trap is a U-

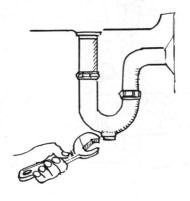

shaped section of pipe put there to prevent sewer gases from invading the home. It may or may not be equipped with a clean-out plug that can be unscrewed to remove the obstruction.

The simplest way to handle a clogged drain is to catch it early. When water drains slowly from a sink or tub, it is a sign that an obstruction exists. Bathroom sinks are often equipped with a removable lint trap that will catch hair, bits of soap, and other matter. This should be taken out and cleaned before anything else is done.

A rubber force cup, or "plumber's friend," can be used to free moderate blockage of tub, sink, or toilet. To work this the rubber cup is set squarely over the drain opening and the handle is pumped up and down vigorously. In order to create the necessary suction there should be enough water in the fixture to cover the plunger head. It helps to plug the overflow outlet with a wet rag, when this is possible. Run or flush plenty of water down the drain once the obstruction has been dislodged.

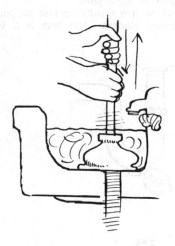

If the trap has an access plug, unscrew this and poke a stiff wire around inside the pipe to break up or extract the obstruction. Place a pan or bucket underneath to catch water spills. If no plug exists, loosen the two nuts at either end of the trap and remove the entire section. (Some traps can be disconnected simply by applying downward pressure by hand.) Run the wire through the trap and also into the exposed ends of fixed pipe sections.

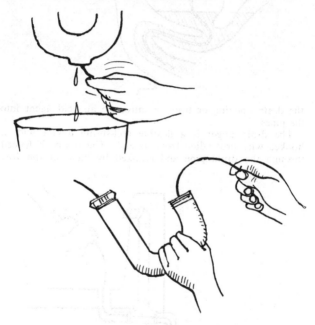

If the blockage is further along inside the pipe, or in tubs or toilets where the trap is not accessible, it will be necessary to run a flexible metal snake (drain auger) through

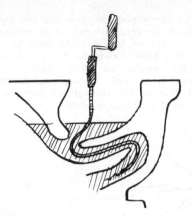

the drain opening or trap, or introduce an acid agent into the pipes.

The drain auger is a flexible coil-spring device with a hooked wire protruding from its end. The device is forced through the drain pipe and cranked by hand at the free

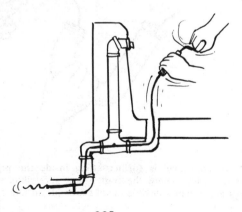

end so that the tip will rotate and bite into an obstruction. It is easier to use if one person holds the snake in position while another does the cranking. A snake about 4 to 6 feet in length is a handy addition to your tool chest. Longer ones, if needed, can be rented.

Grease and soap clinging to a pipe can sometimes be removed by flushing with hot water. Lye, or lye mixed with a small amount of aluminum shavings, may also be used. When water is added to the mixture, the violent gas-forming reaction and production of heat that takes place loosens the grease and soap so that they can be flushed away. Use cold water only. Chemical cleaners should not be used in pipes that are completely stopped-up, because they must be brought into direct contact with the stoppage to be effective. Handle the material with extreme care and follow the directions on the container. If lye spills on hands or clothing, wash with cold water immediately. If any gets into your eyes, flush with cold water and call a doctor.

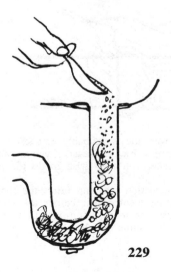

Clogged Sewer Lines

When one or more drains are clogged at the same time, or if the above methods fail to correct blockage, the trouble may be due to obstructions in the sewer line or possibly a flooded cesspool or septic tank, if you are not connected to city sewerage. When a home waste unit backs up it is usually first noticed at the utility drains closest to ground level. Have the cesspool or septic tank checked right away and emptied, if necessary.

Blockage in a sewer line may be caused by collected waste or foreign matter at some point in the underground pipe or by surrounding tree roots that have taken over. Roots will enter fine cracks in certain pipe materials and continue to grow inside the pipe until they form an almost solid mass. This can take place at a single point, or along a great length of an older pipe.

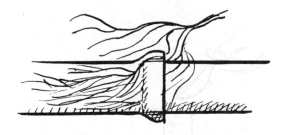

Clearing a plugged sewer line is probably best left to a plumber, for it can be tiring work. However, if you are able to hire a heavy-duty snake, you may wish to do the job yourself.

To clear a simple obstruction you can insert the snake through the clean-out plug located just before the waste line exits from the house. It may be possible to rent a motorized unit and thus save some muscle.

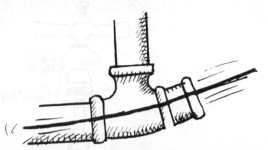

Tree roots are another matter. An auger with special cutting blades at the end must be used. There are companies that specialize in such work, or it may be possible in your community to rent the equipment. A less sure method of destroying the roots is to pour a solution of copper sulphate, sold in hardware stores, into the sewer line. Several applications may be necessary and the results are not always guaranteed.

Leaking and Noisy Faucets

Faucet problems around the home can be corrected with little difficulty. The only tools you will need are a screwdriver and wrench, or waterpump pliers. You should also have on hand an assortment of disc or faucet and packing washers or, for older faucets, a quantity of packing material.

Drips and noises are usually caused by a worn or defective faucet washer. This washer is screwed to the end of the valve stem and provides a tight seal against the flow opening when the faucet handle is closed. If the washer becomes worn, water will leak out no matter how tightly you close the tap.

In some cases there is a resounding "thunk" followed by a diminution of water flow after the tap is opened. The

231

Cap nut

Packing

Washer

fault here is that the screw that holds the washer to the valve stem has become loose. It should be tightened or replaced, if damaged (brass screws are supplied with replacement washers), and a new washer installed as well.

When water dribbles out from beneath the handle it is a sign that the packing is worn or the packing nut is loose. Sometimes tightening the nut a quarter-turn or so will correct the problem. Otherwise new packing must be installed.

Water dribbles. Needs new packing

To replace a washer or install new packing, first shut off the water supply to the system. The water can be turned off at the main supply valve or, if one is provided, at the supply valve for the particular fixture.

A screw usually holds the handle in place. Remove this and lift off the handle, rocking it up and down to loosen it. Next you must remove the packing nut underneath. On some decorative units this nut may be concealed beneath a chrome housing, which must first be removed. On bath fixtures it may be necessary to remove other types of decorative trim.

Loosen the nut with wrench or pliers and lift it off to expose the packing material or washer. If the nut is plated, slip a section of cloth around the jaws of the tool to avoid scratching the finish. Remove the packing and replace the handle temporarily so that you can screw the entire valve assembly out of the faucet. The old washer may now be

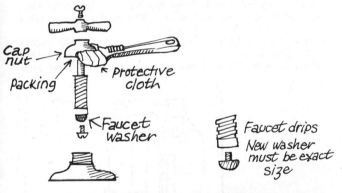

unscrewed and pried off with the tip of a knife. The replacement washer must fit exactly into the receptacle at the stem bottom. Screw it into place tightly and replace the assembly. Install new packing and replace the packing nut, then any decorative trim and the handle.

233

When disc washers wear out frequently, the fault is in the metal seat against which the washer presses. The seat is worn or rough and must be resurfaced or replaced. Dressing kits are available at low cost in any hardware store. The dressing tool is inserted in place of the stem assembly, then rotated to resurface the face of the seat.

Toilet Tank Troubles

Repairs to the toilet flush mechanism require little effort or expertise. Usually a simple adjustment will take care of most problems. Tank components are easily accessible and replacement parts are standardized.

On a typical mechanism, water is admitted to the tank through an inlet valve connected by a steel rod to the float ball. When the ball rises to the proper level, the valve is shut off. A tube leads from the valve to the bowl refill tube to fill the bowl with water. The refill tube also takes care of any overflow in the tank.

When the toilet is flushed, a metal arm lifts the rubber ball valve from its seat. This allows the collected tank water to rush into the bowl, where gravity and water pres-

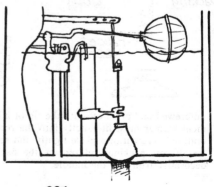

sure carry it vigorously down the drain. At this point the inlet valve takes over and the ball valve slides back down on its seat, preventing further passage of water until the next flushing. The tank then refills, and the inlet valve shuts off.

The most common disorder experienced with flush mechanisms is the continuous trickle of water into the bowl. This usually happens when the ball valve does not seat squarely over the bowl filler opening. The first thing you

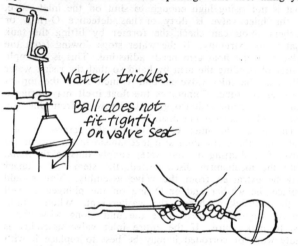

Water trickles.

Ball does not
fit tightly
on valve seat

should check is the lift rod that attaches to the ball valve. The lower link of this metal rod must be straight and its action within the fixed guide arm smooth and unimpaired. If bent it will prevent the valve from seating properly.

You can attempt to straighten the rod by hand, but it is best to replace it with a new one, first disconnecting it from the ball valve. Also check the condition of the ball valve itself. Age may have deteriorated it so that it does not make a tight seal.

235

To replace rod or valve, flush the water from the tank and tie or fix the float arm at its highest position so that it does not release more water into the tank. (Or you can shut off the water supply outside the tank.) Before installing a new ball valve, give the metal seat a going over with steel wool. Check that the stem guide is positioned exactly over the ball seat, shifting it if necessary by loosening the set screws that hold it in place.

If the trouble is not at these points, then either the tank float is not rising high enough to shut off the inlet valve, or the inlet valve is dirty or has defective O-rings or washers. You can check the former by lifting the tank float to its extremity. If the water stops flowing from the valve only the float arm needs adjusting. This is a simple matter of bending the arm by hand so that the rising water will shut the inlet valve around 1 inch from the top of the overflow tube. Sometimes the float itself may spring a leak and become waterlogged. Unscrew it from the rod and install a replacement float.

To service the inlet valve, loosen the screws or pins that retain the entire float arm mechanism to the top of the valve, first shutting off the water supply outside the tank. With the mechanism disconnected, the stem and plunger may be extracted from the valve assembly. You should replace the washer and/or O-ring on the plunger as well as the ballcock washer at the washer seat. When obtaining replacement washers, take the unit along with you—just to make sure. If the entire inlet valve assembly is badly worn or corroded it may be best to replace it with a new assembly.

Stopping Pipe Leaks

Because of the obvious damage they can cause, leaks in pipes should be corrected as soon as they are noticed. There are a number of temporary or permanent repairs you can make until a plumber is available (and one should be called immediately if the section of pipe at fault is badly damaged and you are not prepared or equipped to replace it yourself).

The first thing you must do is drain the pipe. Turn off the water at the nearest valve between the leak and water supply and open the faucet nearest the defective pipe. When the water stops flowing from the valve, you can tackle the repair.

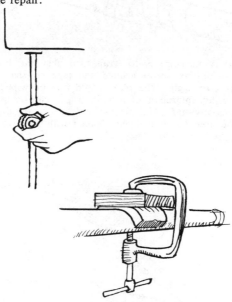

A strictly temporary measure that will stop a leak along the length of a pipe is to clamp a wad of cloth or rubber against the puncture or crack. An ordinary C-clamp and a wood block can be used to hold the material in place. If water pressure in the pipe is not great, another be culled immediately if the section of pipe in fault is badly damaged and you are not prepared or equipped to repair it at once.

The air bottle... cannot do without the tape. Torn off this valve of the venue side force... the tap... end some plastic tape may resolve quite... of delicate tap... which the slow shape itself... where there you can

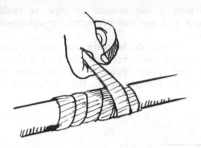

temporary measure is to wrap tape over the leak point. Wrap a double spiral around the pipe so that the tape can stick to itself. The pipe should first be wiped dry.

A permanent repair of a pinhole leak can be made with epoxy compound. The pipe should be dry on the outside and the area to be patched cleaned with steel wool. Mix

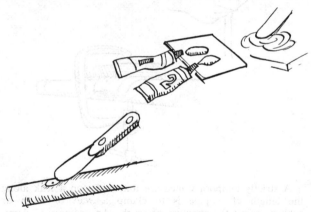

the epoxy and hardener and spread a reasonable quantity over the prepared area. If a "5-minute" epoxy is used, you can turn the water on all that much quicker.

Another method that can be used also for larger cracks (within reason) along a pipe is to obtain a pipe clamp, available in hardware and plumbing supply stores. The pipe is first cleaned, then a cut section of inner tube or rubber mat is wrapped around the damaged section. The pipe clamp is then tightly belted into place to form a permanent seal.

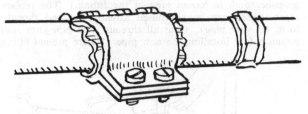

Epoxy compound can also be used to stop leaks at steel pipe joints and fittings.

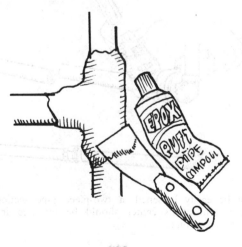

An old or badly corroded section of pipe may not stand up under this kind of repair, and you can count on more trouble later. The only solution is to replace the pipe. Cut the pipe through at its center with a hacksaw. The cut pipe can then be unscrewed at the nearest joint, using two wrenches, one to hold the pipe, the other to hold the fitting to which it is attached. (For copper pipe, use a propane torch to loosen pipe at the fitting.) The replacement section can be purchased already cut and threaded to fit (if steel pipe). Coat all threads with pipe-joint compound before installing the new pipe. Where present fittings

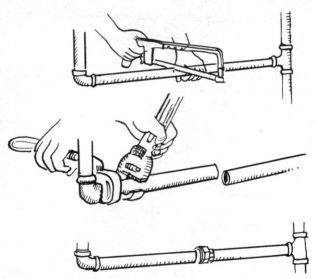

cannot be easily loosened, a two-piece pipe section with a union joint at its center should be installed in place of the damaged pipe.

240

Sweating and Frozen Pipes

Weather extremes can cause water lines to act up. In hot weather, the amount of condensation formed on a cold water pipe can approach leak proportions. When ice-skating weather rolls around, water in lines that run through colder parts of the home (such as an uninsulated crawl space) can freeze and cause pipes to burst.

In both cases the trouble can be avoided by proper insulation of the pipes. A number of insulating materials are available for the purpose, as well as insulators to prevent heat loss from water heaters and hot water pipes. Some are in strip form and can be wrapped around the pipe. Another type is installed in sleeve sections. Yet another can be applied to the pipe with a brush. All are easy to install, and are readily available in hardware and plumbing supply stores.

Before attempting to thaw a frozen pipe, shut off the water supply before the frozen section and open the first faucet after it.

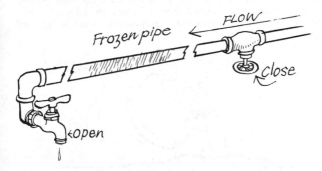

You should never apply direct, intense heat—steam produced within the pipe could create an explosion. A small propane torch may be used, but the flame should be

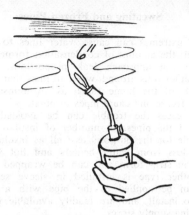

held 6 inches or so from the pipe, and never in one fixed spot.

The safest thawing method is to wrap cloth or towel around the frozen pipe and soak the material with boiling water. When the opened faucet begins to drip, you will know you have succeeded. A portable electric radiant

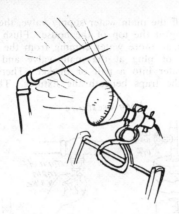

heater can be used as well. If the frozen pipe is covered by plaster or wallboard, a portable heater or sun lamp may provide the necessary heat to thaw it. The appliance should be placed no closer than 6 inches to the wall, however.

A pipe that is cracked or burst because of freezing should be patched or replaced, as described earlier in "Stopping Pipe Leaks."

When you leave your house for any extended period during the winter season you should provide for a minimum of heat from the heating system—that is, if someone can keep an eye on it. Otherwise (as in a summer cottage), the safest approach is to drain all water from the pipes.

Long absence from home. Drain all water systems

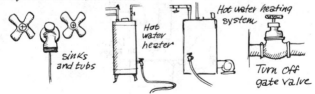

sinks
and tubs

Hot
water
heater

Hot water heating
system

Turn off
gate valve

First shut off the main water supply valve, then open all faucets, starting at the top of the house. Flush all toilets. When there is no more water coming from the taps, open the draincock or plug at the main valve and drain the rest of the water into a pail or bucket. There will still be water in the traps beneath the fixtures. This can be

Long Vacations

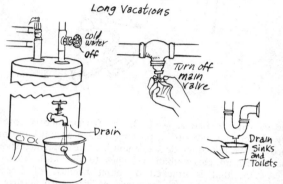

removed by unscrewing the trap cleanout plug or, if none is provided, by disconnecting the trap. On toilets, secure a sponge to a piece of wire and run this into the trap until all water is sucked up. Keep in mind that there is always a small amount of water collected at the bottom of washing machines and dishwashers. This should be sponged dry to avoid freeze damage to the appliance.

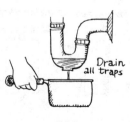

Cesspools and Septic Tanks

Homes that do not tie into public sewer lines empty their waste into a cesspool or septic tank. While the two systems differ in operation, each must be drained and cleaned at regular intervals.

The cesspool is the simplest (or most primitive) in design. Basically it is a hole in the ground, the sides of which are lined with porous masonry blocks. A sewer line from the house pours raw sewage into the hole. Liquids drain off into the soil (sometimes contaminating it and the nearby water supply), while insoluble grease and other matter slowly collects. When the hole is full it must be emptied,

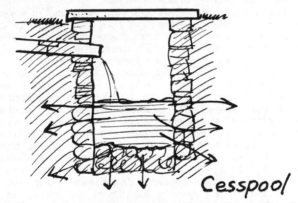

Cesspool

usually once a year or every 18 months. If it is not, the drains will back up into the house and water will flood the area around the cesspool cover. It will also smell a lot.

Sometimes there is more than one hole. There may be a smaller hole or holding chamber before the main cesspool to trap solid matter while liquids pass through to the big hole. This holding chamber can also flood. It should be emptied along with the other.

When a cesspool gets clogged with time and use, or when toilet, bathing, and washing habits change in the household, a new waste hole must be dug. Connected to the old cesspool by a pipe, the new unit will handle the overflow until it, too, becomes clogged with time and use.

The best solution to balky cesspools that must handle year-round waste discharge is to convert to a septic tank system. This is a sealed tank of concrete or steel that uses a natural bacterial action to decompose waste matter and decontaminate water. The tank traps all solid matter in its bottom. This is converted to a sludge by bacteria present in the waste. Water is passed into the soil through one or more pipes buried in the ground depending on capacity and porosity of soil.

Like a cesspool, the septic tank must be drained of sludge in order to prevent blockage and flooding. A trapdoor or manhole is provided for this. Every two years is the recommended interval. Its chief benefit is that it is hygienic and, if not abused, will provide long years of service.

Repairs and cleaning of cesspool or septic tank are best left to the specialist. However, you can help maintain the efficiency of the system by exercising some control over what goes into it. Grease causes the most trouble with pipes and tanks. On a septic unit, grease will retard bacterial action as well as help clog pipes and drains. Make sure all kitchen and bath drains are able to filter out solid matter. Pouring in coffee grounds, despite what some may believe, is not a good idea. Adjust household habits, if need be, to dispose of facial tissues, "disposable" baby diapers, and sanitary napkins in the garbage can instead of down the toilet. Never allow water to drain from swimming pool or rainspouts into the system, as this will quickly flood the holding tank.

CHAPTER 13

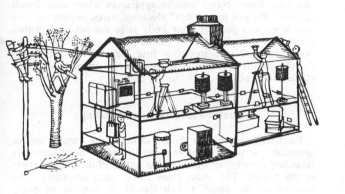

Electricity

Small electrical repairs around the home can be tackled with safety and confidence if you know how to trace and correct the trouble and take some elementary precautions. Common sense and local building codes dictate that major repair and installation of wiring be left to the licensed electrician.

But there are many simple repairs you should be prepared to handle yourself. When a fuse blows, for example, you can trace the cause and correct it so that the system operates properly. Doorbells and chimes that refuse to work can be handled easily if you know how to troubleshoot the circuit. Balky light switches can be replaced in short order. Electric cords and plugs can be replaced without trouble. You can install supplementary outlets without fear

247

of shorts or overload if you know how much your electrical system can handle.

A word of caution. Electricity can hurt. It can kill. It can start fires. Never handle appliances when your hands are wet. Do not touch "hot" electrical wires, outlets, or fuse box when any part of your body is in contact with water, damp walls or floor, or a plumbing fixture. Shut off the power first. Never install a fuse higher than that rated for the circuit. And if you smell smoke, immediately turn off the main power supply to the home.

Circuit Protection and Loading

Electricity enters the home through the "main service entrance," a box containing one or more heavy-capacity fuses and a switch or other means to cut off the entire supply to the home. The main fuses rarely need attention. The location of the cutoff switch should be familiar to every member of the household in case of emergency (often, the main fuse section is simply pulled out to cut off power). Power is routed through a "branch-distribution box" to individual circuits throughout the home, each of which is protected by a fuse or circuit breaker. These circuit protectors shut off power to the individual circuit when there is an overload condition or when bare wires somewhere in the circuit or appliance touch and create a "short."

The most common fuse is a glass-faced unit that screws into the fuse panel. A metal element, visible through the window of the fuse, burns and breaks when one of the above conditions exists and interrupts power to the circuit. The only way to restore power is to install a new fuse. Circuit breakers, on the other hand, simply switch themselves to the "off" position, and need only to be manually switched "on." These devices are a series of switches on the power panel and are found usually in newer homes. There are accessory circuit breakers available that can be screwed into a fuse panel to replace a fuse.

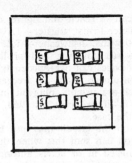

In no case should power be restored to the circuit until the overload or short that caused it to shut off is eliminated or corrected. Otherwise the circuit will just continue blowing.

The usual trouble is overload due to use of too many appliances plugged into the same circuit. Most fuses are rated at 15 amperes, which provides a maximum of 1,800 watts of power consumption. When the power draw of several appliances exceeds this figure, the fuse will blow to prevent wires from overheating.

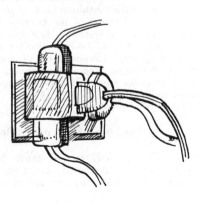

If you think it is difficult to reach that figure, consider the following average appliance loads: toaster—1,100 watts; vacuum cleaner—up to 700 watts; dishwasher—1,250 watts. And so on. It is easy to see how use and proliferation of modern appliances and devices can overburden the house wiring. Heavy power consumers such as freezer, dishwasher, and air conditioner are usually plugged into individual circuits of their own—if properly installed, that is. In many homes this is not the case.

Sometimes an overload on the circuit may not be great enough to blow a fuse. You can spot this when the lights dim as an appliance ·is plugged in or starts automatically. While this condition may not be immediately hazardous, it can impair the efficiency of the appliance because it is not getting enough voltage. And it can burn out electric motors.

The only solution to an overloaded circuit is to plug the offenders into another, less-burdened circuit. You must never replace the fuse with one of a higher rating; the wiring will heat up and may well start a fire. For the same reason you must never stick a penny or piece of tin foil in the fuse receptacle. If you do, and the house catches fire, your insurance company will turn a deaf ear.

You can figure the maximum load on any circuit by multiplying the ampere rating of the circuit's fuse by 120 (the voltage rating of the system). This gives you a figure in watts, e.g., 15 amps x 120 volts = 1,800 watts. Then add up the number of watts consumed by all appliances that may be used at the same time in that circuit. A plate on the appliance gives the figure. If only an ampere rating is supplied, multiply by 120.

Tracking a Short or Overload

Rarely will electricity to the entire home be cut off unless a storm has disrupted service or the main fuses have blown. In both cases you are at the mercy of the power company or electrician (it is best not to tamper with the main fuses). Candlelight can be fun for very short periods.

When parts of the house lose power you will have to determine the cause of failure and correct it. Unless the trouble is immediately apparent, you should unplug all lights and appliances in the defective circuit before attempting to replace a blown fuse or reset a circuit breaker. A blown fuse will be apparent from its blackened condition on the glass face; a circuit breaker will be in the "off" position.

Always shut off the main power before trying to replace a fuse. It is the only safe way. If the power box is in a basement with a damp floor, make sure you stand on a wood box or grating. A rubber mat will also do. Take a

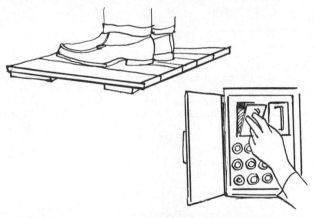

flashlight along and turn off the main service switch at the side of the fuse panel. Some panels will not have a switch. Instead, the main fuses are hidden behind a smaller, labeled panel with a hinged handle on the cover. Pulling out this panel from the main panel shuts off all power to the house.

Replace the fuse with one of the same rating or reset the circuit breaker and restore power. If the circuit blows

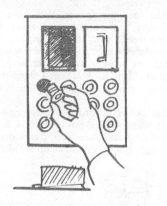 

again, and you have unplugged all appliances, there is a short in the internal wiring and an electrician should be called. If the circuit stays open you can now proceed to look for the cause. First determine the total power draw of appliances used at the same time in that circuit. If the draw exceeds what the circuit can handle you will have to switch one or more appliances to another circuit or make sure they are not all turned on at the same time.

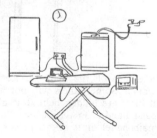

If the draw is within acceptable limits, then the trouble is a short in one of the appliances. Check for frayed insulation or loose plugs that might permit bare wires to

come in contact with each other. Replace or repair these, as required. If the fault is not readily visible you can isolate the defective appliance by plugging each electric unit, one by one, until the circuit again blows. Do not use that appliance again until the short is corrected.

Replacing a Wall Switch

When a light switch fails because of wear the only thing you can do is replace it. This is simple to do as long as you first turn off the current in that circuit by either closing the power main or opening the circuit breaker to that section (if in doubt, turn off all power).

The two most common switches found in homes are the single-pole—a simple two-wire switch—and the three-way, usually found in hallways or garages where it is desirable ~~to~~ same light from two different locations. Three wires a.e connected to this type of switch.

Remove the screws that hold the switch cover in place

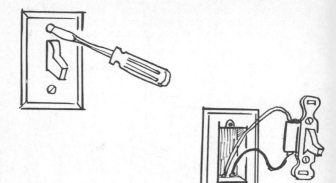

and remove the cover. Then take out the two screws holding the switch to the recessed metal box. Extract the switch assembly and observe how the two or three wires are mounted to the contact screws. They should be reconnected to the new switch in the same order.

Clockwise

Disconnect the wires and wrap each in a clockwise loop around the contact screws of the new switch. (Just loosen these screws, as they can be difficult to replace once they are removed.) Secure the wires, then remount the switch in its receptacle and replace the cover. Power may then be restored.

Switch assemblies are standardized and you will have no difficulty finding a replacement to fit the receptacle and wiring.

Even if a switch is not defective you may wish to replace it for cosmetic or convenience reasons. In sick room or nursery a silent mercury switch may be desirable. In kitchen, laundry room, or bath a push-type switch will permit you to actuate it with free parts of your body when your hands are full. In living room or den, a rheostat switch will permit dimming control of lights for dramatic effects. All can be easily installed as described above.

Appliance Cords and Plugs

Wear and damage to appliance cords and plugs are common occurances in the home, usually as the result of abuse rather than age. An appliance is disconnected with a yank on the cord instead of a tug on the plug. Wires are routed under rugs where there is much foot traffic, or around hot radiators. Or they may be casually stapled to woodwork. These are the most common causes of short circuits and nasty shocks.

DONT'S

You should inspect appliance cords regularly for signs of frayed, cracked, or broken insulation, and check plugs for damaged prongs and loose terminal connections. When any of these conditions exist, the cord or plug must be replaced.

It is important that the replacement match the appliance to which it is being fitted. Lamps, radios, televisions, and other low-power devices can use standard lightweight cord and any standard rubber or plastic replacement plug. Heavy-duty braided or rubber cord should be used for vacuum cleaners, power tools, outdoor extension lamps, and large appliances. Toasters, irons, hot plates, and any heating appliance should have special heat-resistant cord—to use any other type is to invite trouble.

The most common type of plug has terminal screws to which the cord wires are attached. Yanking a cord to remove the plug from the outlet usually results in the insulation just behind the plug fraying or cracking, or its terminal connections coming loose. If the plug and cord look intact otherwise, and prongs and insulation are in good condition, simply disconnect the cord at the terminals and pull it through the plug until you reach insulation that is intact.

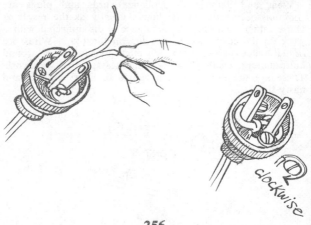

clockwise

Cut the cord at this point, then separate the two wires to a length of about 1½ inches. With a sharp knife strip ½ inch of insulation from each end, taking care not to cut through the wire. Twist the wire ends so there are no loose strands. Loop each wire around a prong and wrap the wire around the terminal screws in the same direction the screw will be tightened.

Some plugs are sealed and have the cord wires soldered directly to the prongs. In this case you will have to cut off the plug and install a new one.

For heavy-duty plugs and cords with braided or heavy rubber insulation, cut about 3 inches of the cord's outer insulating material but leave the inside insulation for the individual wires intact. You must then tie the two ends into an "underwriters' knot," which will fit snugly into the base

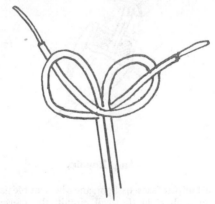

of the plug. This is designed to prevent wires from pulling loose from the terminals when subjected to sudden tugs, as they would be with any heavy-duty appliance that has to be moved around. Once the knot has been made and tested for fit, strip ½ inch of insulation from the wire ends and connect as described above. It is a good idea to use

257

the underwriters' knot on any appliance that has a plug large enough to accommodate the knot.

With light-duty parallel cord, simple snap-on plugs may be used. These are fitted firmly over the end of the unstripped cord; movable prongs pierce the insulation to make contact with the wire, as well as to provide a firm grip.

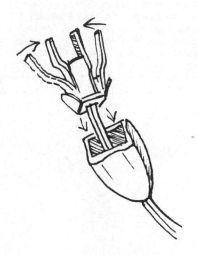

Lamp Repairs

When a lamp refuses to light and the trouble is not with the bulb or a short in the wall circuit, the cause is either the plug, the lamp wire, or the socket. First check the plug for good contact. If it fits loosely in the wall outlet, try bending the prongs apart a bit. If the lamp does not light, check for loose wires at the plug terminals. If the plug prongs are loose or if the plug looks in any way doubtful, replace the plug, as described previously.

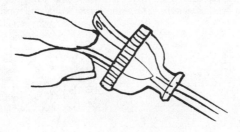

Sockets rarely need replacement, but if they incorporate a switching device the switch may wear with use, and the entire socket must be replaced. Unplug the lamp and remove the bulb. The socket assembly is in two parts, a cap fixed to the lamp base and a brass shell that snaps onto that. Inside are a combined switch and socket plus a cardboard or fiber liner that protects against short circuits.

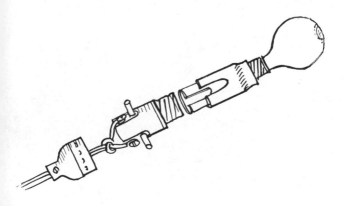

Snap off the shell by pressing at the point indicated at the base of the shell, then remove it and the liner to gain access to the switch. Disconnect the wires and remove the

switch. The cap can be left in place and the other parts replaced as an assembly, available in any hardware outlet.

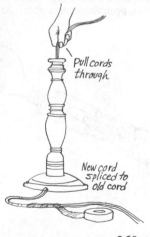

Pull cords through

New cord spliced to old cord

It is often difficult, if not downright impossible, to thread a new cord into a lamp by probing, particularly on tall floor units. A simple solution is to cut or disconnect the plug of the old wire and attach one end of the new wire to that. Make the temporary splice as secure and slim as possible. Disconnect the old cord at the lamp socket and pull gently until the new cord emerges through the fixed socket cap. Connect to the socket or switch and replace the shell. Then attach a new plug.

Doorbells and Chimes

When a bell or chime refuses to sound, the first thing you should check is the button. Remove the pushbutton and inspect for loose connections. If all are tight, either bridge the button terminals with a piece of wire or paper clip or disconnect the wires and touch the bare ends together. (The maximum voltage across the terminals is 24 volts, probably less, so do not worry about shocks.)

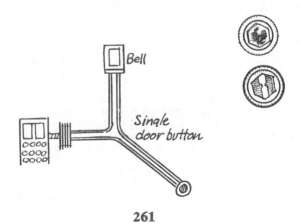

261

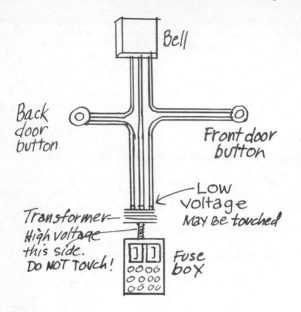

Bell

Back door button

Front door button

Low voltage May Be touched

Transformer—High voltage this side. DO NOT TOUCH!

Fuse box

If the bell sounds, the trouble is in the button and it should be replaced. If it does not sound, you should check the power supply, a transformer usually wired alongside the main fuse box. The *output* terminals of the transformer can be bridged with a screwdriver. (Never touch *input* terminals—these are wired to the house 110-120 volt current, and can give a severe shock.) If sparks appear, power is coming through and you should look elsewhere.

If voltage is not coming through the transformer, either the fuse to the circuit is blown or the transformer has burned out.

If there is power, the next thing you should check is the chime or bell. Remove the cover or housing and look for dirty or sticking parts and broken connections. Sand contact points if they appear pitted or corroded. With chimes, check for free operation of the small rods that move to strike the chime bars. Clean as required.

When bell or chimes,pushbuttons and power supply check out and all visible connections are tight, the trouble is in the wiring. Repair in this case is best left to the electrician.

CHAPTER **14**

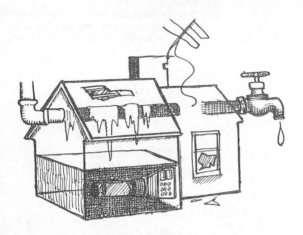

In Case of Emergency
What To Do Until
The Repairman
Comes

When emergency situations occur in the home, you should be prepared to administer "first aid" until such time as you can permanently repair the fault or have it corrected by a professional. Quick action on your part can prevent costly damage to materials, furnishings, and equipment.

264

A roof leak during monsoonlike periods, for example, should be stopped at once to avoid water damage to walls and ceilings. If a hot water heating system breaks down for any length of time, you must take steps to see that water pipes do not freeze and burst. When shorts or overloads occur in the electrical system, you should know what safety procedures to follow until the electrician comes.

Plumbing

Pipe Leaks

Shut off the flow valve before the leak point and open the faucet nearest the defect to drain water from the pipe. A temporary repair can be made by wrapping tape around the pipe in a double spiral. Or wrap a strip of rubber around the pipe and secure it with a pipe clamp. A C-clamp and a block of wood may also be used to press a wad of cloth or rubber against the opening.

When a pipe joint comes apart, first turn off the water at the nearest valve or at the main intake point. A short piece of hose can be used to reconnect the two pieces temporarily until permanent repairs can be made. Use pipe clamps to secure the hose.

Exposure to Cold

If the heating system should break down, or a power blackout occur, water pipes must be protected from freezing. Opening the taps a bit will help, since flowing water is less likely to freeze. In a pinch, pipes in the coldest parts of the house—the basement or an uninsulated crawl space—can be wrapped loosely with several sheets of newspaper overlapped and tied at the ends; this will serve as temporary insulation.

If the electrical power or heating system is off for a

prolonged period of time in subfreezing weather, the plumbing system should be completely drained. A drain valve is usually provided at the low point of the supply piping for this purpose. Pumps, storage tanks, hot water tanks, toilet tanks, hot water and steam heating systems, and other water-system appliances or accessories should also be drained. Put antifreeze in all fixture and drain traps.

Frozen Pipes

The best method of thawing water that has frozen inside pipes is to apply an electric heating cable to the pipes. Wrap the cable around so that the entire length of the pipe can be thawed at one time. Leave the cable in place to supply continuous heat during extremely cold weather.

A propane torch can also be used, but exercise extreme caution. Never concentrate the torch's heat on a single section of pipe; the water within may become hot enough

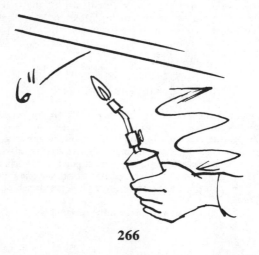

to generate steam under pressure and rupture the pipe. Keep the torch moving and at a safe distance from the pipe. Also be careful that the flame does not scorch or set fire to surrounding wood framing.

A safer method of thawing frozen pipes is to cover them with rags and then pour hot water over the rags. What-

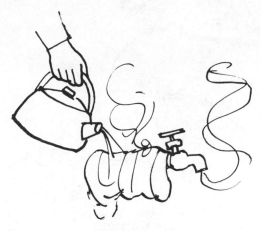

ever method you use, first open a faucet beyond the frozen point, then begin the thawing operation there. The open faucet will permit steam to escape, thus reducing the chance of the buildup of dangerous pressure. Do not allow the steam to condense and refreeze before it reaches the faucet.

Hot-Water Tank Rumbles

This is likely a sign of overheating that could lead to the development of explosive pressure. (Another indication of overheating is hot water backing up in the cold water

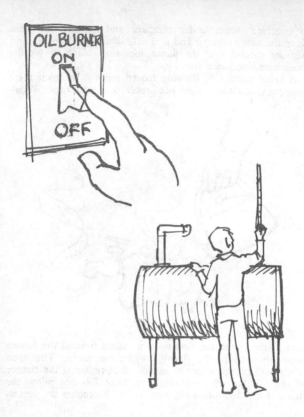

supply pipe.) Shut off the burner immediately. Be sure that the pressure-relief valve is operative, then check the temperature of the water at the nearest outlet with a thermometer. If the temperature is above that for which the tank's thermostat is set, check the burner cutoff control. If you cannot find and correct the trouble, call the plumber.

Turn off the valve on the pipe leading into the toilet tank. If there is no valve there, turn off the main supply valve. Remove the top of the tank to see if any parts of the mechanism are broken, rusted, or jammed. Check for and remove stoppage in bowl outlet and drain line from bowl to sewer or septic tank. If you cannot find the trouble right away, call the plumber.

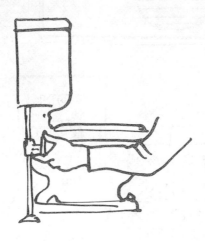

Electricity

Overheated Wires

When your nose detects the unmistakable odor of burning insulation you must act quickly. If the trouble is obviously in an appliance, unplug it at once. Should the smell seem

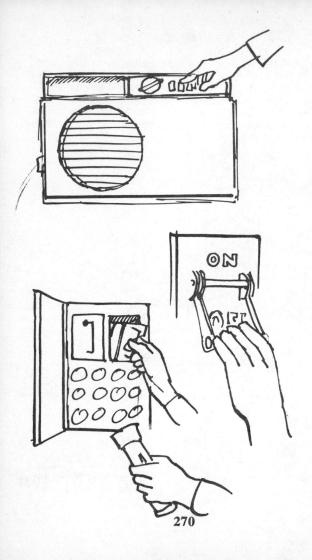

270

to originate in the house wiring, immediately cut off the main power at the fuse box (take along a flashlight to avoid fumbling around in the dark). If you know from which circuit the smell is coming, pull the fuse to that circuit or shut off the circuit breaker. If you are not sure, keep the main power off until the electrician comes.

Partial Blackout

If a room or portion of the house is plunged into darkness, immediately unplug all appliances in the affected circuit, then check for a burned-out fuse at the fuse box. Turn

off the main power before replacing the fuse, and be sure to use one of the same rating. (If your system is equipped with circuit breakers, simply switch the breaker to "on.") If the fuse immediately burns out (or the circuit breaker again goes off) there is a short in the circuit and power should be left off until an electrician can repair it. If the fuse remains intact, check for a short in one of the appliances or for an overload condition (see Chapter 13).

Total Blackout

This may be caused by one or more of the main house fuses blowing, in which case the utility company should be called to correct the situation. Usually, however, the cause of the blackout is outside the house (you can look around at the neighbor's homes to see if they are also in the dark) and you simply have to wait. When this happens, turn off the oil burner emergency switch as well as any other appliances that are on when the failure occurs. This will avoid possible damage to the burner and appliance motors because of low voltage when power is restored. Once power is fully flowing, appliances can be turned on again.

If power is out for a lengthy period in cold weather, take precautions outlined in the section on "Plumbing."

Heating

Furnace Failure

Check the main switch; it may have been turned off accidentally. Check for a blown fuse or circuit breaker.

Check the thermostat to see if it has been turned down; remove the cover to see if dirt or dust is clogging the contacts. Check the fuel supply (this applies mostly to oil-fired systems, but it is conceivable that a gas intake valve may mistakenly be turned off).

Follow the troubleshooting procedures outlined in Chapter 11 for various types of heating systems. If the problem is not easy to pinpoint or repair, do not delay calling the serviceman.

When You Smell Gas

Get everybody out of the house—the stronger the smell, the greater the urgency. If possible, turn the thermostat way down so that the furnace does not come on, possibly setting off an explosion. Call the gas company, immediately, from a neighbor's phone if possible. If this is not practical and the gas smell is not too strong, hold a handkerchief over your nose and go back into the house, dial the operator and tell her the trouble, and get back outside immediately. Do not go back into the house again until the gas company servicemen have repaired the leak.

Storm Damage

Broken Windows

When a window breaks during a storm, it is often impractical or impossible to repair it immediately. As a stopgap measure, staple a large piece of plastic sheet to the casement, sides, and sill. Clear plastic should be a part of every homeowner's emergency repair kit, but if none

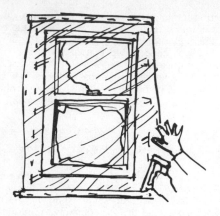

is available, cover the window with any material that will keep out the elements—plywood, hardboard, or even an old blanket.

Roof Leaks

High winds often rip loose roof shingles, allowing water to seep through the roof and into the attic. Soon, ceilings

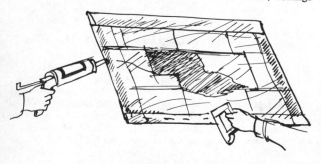

and walls show evidence of water damage. If you can get onto the roof but the weather prevents you from making a permanent repair by replacing the damaged or missing shingles, cover the affected area with a plastic or rubber sheet, slipping it underneath the shingles above it and stapling the ends down. Caulk around the edges of the sheet to prevent water from being driven under it.

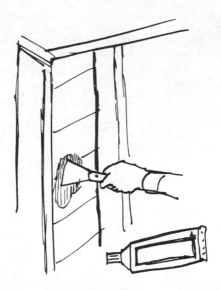

When ice or snow conditions do not allow you to correct the problem from above, you can locate the leak in an exposed attic or crawl space. Apply waterproof sealer from a can or tube (available at any hardware store, this too should be in your "first aid" kit), working it well into and around the area to keep out water at least until the storm abates. Make permanent repairs as soon as possible.

Heavy accumulations of ice or snow, or extremely high winds, can cause power lines to snap. Such broken lines are extremely dangerous and should never be closely approached.

As soon as you spot a downed line (your house power will probably fail), report it immediately to the utility company. During a storm, however, when many power lines may be down and the roads are snow-clogged and icy, it may be some time before a repair crew will be on the scene. Steps should be taken to warn passersby.

On whatever material is available (hardboard, plywood, heavy cardboard), make a sign reading something like: "DANGER! LIVE WIRE! KEEP AWAY!" The sign should be as large as possible, preferably a white background with large, bold printing in red or black. Tack the sign to a stake and drive the stake into the ground a considerable distance from the wire. If necessary, make more signs to face in all possible directions of approach to the danger area.

If possible, blockade the danger area. Boards placed across sawhorses will be effective, if these are available. Or drive stakes into the ground and rope off the area, just as you would a newly seeded lawn. Strips of cloth tied to the rope or string will make it more visible. At night, set off the area with warning lights. Flares can be used, although most types burn for relatively short periods. Kerosene lanterns, placed where they cannot be missed by passersby, are better.

In Case of Fire

Shout "Fire!" as loudly as possible. Arouse everyone immediately and get them outside. *Do not linger to save possessions!*

Call the fire department. In most cases, you simply need dial the operator. Clearly give her your address.

If the fire is confined to a small area and you have a safe and sure exit available, use any available extinguisher to fight the flames until the firemen arrive. But be certain you know what you are doing (an obvious example: do not use water to try to douse a grease fire—it will only spread the flames), and skip this step completely unless your own safety and that of your family is assured.

Some of these suggestions seem absurdly elementary, but they bear endless repeating. Too often a person, in the panic of the moment, will try to extinguish a fire himself. By the time he realizes the futility of this and calls the fire department, it may be too late. Worse yet, members of the family in other parts of the house who have not been warned in time may be trapped.

The real key to avoiding a disaster is prevention. Make sure that every member of the family knows exactly what to do in an emergency. Have an alternate escape route for every room. Rooms on upper floors should have windows that are easily opened. Rope ladders should be placed in all "dead-end" rooms, and children should be well versed in their use.

These are the "ounces of prevention" that save lives.

CHAPTER 15

Your Regular Maintenance Program: A Calendar Checklist

Preventive maintenance is the key to proper home care and comfort. It will also mean a real dollar saving by helping you spot and head off little problems before they can grow into big ones. A regular program of checks and

279

services means that you can avoid the anxiety of dealing with the inevitable household problems on an emergency basis.

The checklist given here suggests convenient times of the year to tackle the various parts of the home and its equipment. The schedule is, of course, flexible, but its point is firm: by spreading checks and services throughout the year and making them on a planned, regular basis, you will be sure of giving every part of your home the attention it needs and deserves. The page references will direct you to detailed discussions of the procedures involved.

Spring

Walks and Driveways

Concrete: repair cracks and breaks; repair any damage caused by frost-heaving
Blacktop: check for water damage, undermining; patch and protect with sealer

Gutters and Downspouts

Gutters: clean out debris and check for blockage, leaks, and misalignment, correcting as required
Downspouts: check for leaks and free flow of drain water; provide splash blocks if needed

Cooling and Ventilating

Air conditioners: get them in shape before the hot weather arrives; clean or replace filters, make sure house wiring is adequate to carry the load; install shade awning over

window unit on sunny side of the house, or reinstall
the unit in a shady area

Attic fan: check the operation of the unit, or consider
the advisability of installing one

Insulation: check attic insulation to make sure it gives
complete coverage; install reflective material if required

Summer

Outside Walls

Siding: repair or replace damaged clapboard or shingles

Masonry: inspect joints in brickwork and tuck point if
necessary; patch cracks or breaks in stucco and concrete; clean off efflorescence

Doors and Windows

Doors: correct misalignment or warping of frame; check
and correct any binding at hinges

Windows: free binding or sticking sashes; renew worn or
broken putty

If you have been diligent in your home-care program all
year, you deserve some time off during the warm weather.
So relax and enjoy the sun.

Fall

Exterior Painting

Check the condition of paint on exterior walls; if a new
paint job is needed, this is the best time to do it

281

Heating Systems

(Check it out before the cold sets in)

Oil burner: clean and oil moving parts; replace fuel nozzle if worn

Boiler: fully or partially flush to remove scale; maintain water level

Radiators: inspect air and shutoff valves; bleed trapped air

Air filters: clean or replace

Blowers and fans: clean; oil bearings; check belts

Smoke pipes and chimneys: clean out soot; inspect for breaks and repair or replace if necessary

Thermostats: check operation; clean dust or dirt from contact points

Weatherproofing

Weatherstripping: check condition of existing material; replace or install new material where needed

Insulation: check for damaged or insufficient insulation in attic; insulate cold floors as needed

Storm windows: check for broken glass; make sure seal between frame and casing is tight

Window and door frames: check for open joints between siding and frame; caulk if necessary

Roofing

Shingles: check for possible leak points; replace loose or damaged shingles

Flashing: inspect for rust or damage; seal with compound, or replace if practicable

Plumbing

Water pipes: make sure insulation around pipes in cold
areas of the house is intact; add insulation where needed

Drains: check for free drainage; have spetic tank or cesspool cleaned if this has not been done recently

Winter

Basement

Check for dampness, cracks in floor and foundation
walls; waterproof or repair as required

Interior Walls and Ceilings

Walls: repair cracks or loose plaster, and breaks or open
seams in wallboard; repair or replace loose or missing
tile

Ceilings: check for plaster damage; repair or install ceiling
tile to conceal badly damaged plaster

Interior Painting

How about sprucing up the house for the holiday season?

Floors and Stairs

Floors: cure squeaks; repair or replace damaged floor
boards; repair or replace damaged or broken floor tiles
or linoleum

Stairs: cure squeaks; tighten loose treads, risers, banisters; turn or replace damaged or worn treads

Electricity

Appliance cords: check for frayed insulation, damaged plugs; repair or replace as required

Circuit loading: determine the capacity of circuits, adjust use of appliances to prevent overloading

Fuse box: check it out and make sure you (and the rest of the family) know how to shut off main power in an emergency; keep a stock of replacement fuses of the correct rating for use in case of shorts or overloads

Glossary

Every profession and every trade has its own language. Whether you are doing your home maintenance yourself or leaving it to the professional, you should be able to speak that language. Here is your dictionary of the most common terms you will encounter when dealing with the repairman or the hardware or building-supply dealer:

Aggregates Sand and gravel that are mixed with cement to make concrete.
Air Space The open area between an inner and outer wall.
Ampere A unit of measurement of electric current.
Anchor Fasteners used to secure timber (as house framing) to masonry (such as a concrete foundation).
Apron The casing or molding under a window sill.
Aquastat A control to regulate the temperature of hot water in a furnace or heater.
Armored Cable Electric wires encased in a metal sheath (BX).
Asbestos Shingles Siding or roofing shingles made of Portland cement and fireproof asbestos.
Awl A pointed tool used to punch holes in various materials.

Backfill Replacement of earth that has been excavated for a trench, pit, or foundation.

Backflow The flow of water into a supply system from any source other than the proper one.

Back Painting Painting the unexposed surface of lumber (such as siding) to prevent moisture penetration.

Backsaw Thin-bladed, fine-toothed saw used for mitering and chamfering.

Balloon Frame Type of construction in which wall studs run from sill plate to roof plate.

Baluster Vertical post on a stair railing.

Balustrade A row of balusters topped by a rail.

Banister A stair rail with its supporting balusters (See Balustrade).

Baseboard Molding that covers the joint between the wall and the floor.

Batt A blanket-type of insulation, usually made of rock wool or fiberglass.

Batten A narrow strip of wood fastening together other pieces of wood.

Beading Narrow, decorative wood molding.

Bevel An angle cut on the edge of a board.

Bibb A faucet with a threaded nozzle for hose attachment.

Board Foot A unit of lumber measurement, 12 inches x 12 inches x 1 inch thick.

Bond The pattern used when laying bricks.

Boxing Mixing paint by pouring from one container to another.

Brace A piece of lumber fastened at an angle to a structure to strengthen that structure.

Brad A small, thin nail.

Brick Veneer An outer layer of brickwork (usually a single or double thickness) over a wall of another material.

Bridging Pieces of wood nailed in X-shape between joists to distribute the floor load; or solid pieces of wood of the same width as the joists fitted between them to serve the same purpose.

Brown Coat The second coat of stucco or plaster.

Building Paper Heavy paper used as a lining between various materials (such as sheating and siding) or as a temporary covering to protect finished work (such as hardwood flooring).

Butter To apply mortar to brick.

Butt Joint A joint where two pieces of wood meet squarely.

BX Cable Flexible metal-sheathed electric wire.

Cap The cement finish atop a chimney or brick wall.

Casement Window A window in which the sash opens on hinges, like a door.

Casing The wood trim around a door or window.

Cement A very fine, powdered mixture of clay and limestone used to mix concrete.

Cesspool A system of sewage disposal.

Chalking Dusting of very fine particles of exterior paint.

Chamfer A beveled surface cut on the corner of a piece of wood.

Check A split or crack in a board.

Check Valve A valve that prevents a return flow of water in a pipe.

Chuck The part of a brace or drill that holds the bit.

Circuit A closed system through which electric power runs from the power source to the point of use and back to the source.

Circuit Breaker An automatic mechanical device that prevents overheating in a circuit due to overloading.

Clapboard A form of board siding.

Clinch To drive a nail through lumber and bend the point back into the wood to prevent its pulling loose.

Collar Beam A board fastened between two rafters to give support.

Column A vertical supporting member.

Common A grade of lumber.

Common Bond A brick pattern composed of a header and several stretcher courses.

Compass Saw Narrow-bladed saw used for curves, circles, and fine cuts.

Concrete Mixture of cement, sand, gravel, or other aggregate and water.

Conductor A material through which electricity flows, usually copper wire. Also, a downspout.

Conduit A pipe through which electric wiring is fed.

Coping Waterproof course atop a masonry wall.

Coping Saw Saw with a very narrow blade that can be turned to cut at various angles.

Corner Bead Metal lath used to reinforce corners.

Cornice Decorative molding placed beneath eaves, or at the top of an interior wall.

Countersink To drive screw heads flush with the surface of the work.

Coupling Plumbing fitting used to join sections of pipe or hose.

Course A layer of shingles or bricks.

Cove Molding Molding with a concave surface.

Creosote Wood or coal tar used as a wood preservative.

Cross-Grain At right angles to the grain of wood.

Dado A groove cut in wood, usually to make a joint.

Dormer A recess built into the side of a roof.

Double-Hung Window A window with movable upper and lower sash.

Downspout Metal pipe to carry water from a roof or gutter to the ground or drainage system. Also called conductor, leader.

Drip Cap Projection along the outside top of a door or window opening to shed water.

Dry Rot Wood decay caused by fungi or dampness.

Dry Well Covered pit lined with gravel or stones to collect drainage water and allow it to seep into the ground.

Eave The part of the roof that extends beyond the walls.

Efflorescence White crust that may appear on bricks, caused by excessive presence of mineral salts.

Emery Paper Abrasive paper or cloth for smoothing surfaces.

End-Matched Lumber Boards tongue-and-grooved on ends and sides.

English Bond A pattern used in laying brick, composed of alternate courses of headers and stretchers.

Epoxy Resin A flexible adhesive especially effective for bonding two different materials.

Escutcheon Metal plate around door knobs and keyholes.

Expansion Bolt Bolt for anchoring in masonry walls.

Expansion Joint Opening between sections of concrete to permit expansion and contraction.

Face The widest plane of a board; the long, narrow exposed portion of a brick.

Fascia Flat, horizontal part of a cornice to which the gutter is usually fastened.

Felt Paper Heavy paper used for insulating and deadening sound.

Ferrule Metal part of a paintbrush that secures the bristles.

Filler Material used to fill wood pores before painting.

Firebrick Brick made to withstand high temperatures for use in furnaces and fireplaces.

Fire Clay Heat-resistant cement used to bond firebrick.

Flashing Material, usually sheet metal or copper, used in roof and wall construction to make the structure watertight.

Flue The opening in a chimney through which smoke passes.

Footing The wide base of a wall, pier, or column.

Foundation The part of a building that supports the superstructure.

Framing The rough lumber structure of a house, before interior and exterior walls, floor, and roof are enclosed.

Frost Line The depth to which earth freezes.

Furring Strips of wood nailed to walls and ceilings to provide an even surface for finishing materials.

Fuse Protective device to interrupt the flow of electric current under conditions of short circuiting or overloading.

Galvanized Metal coated with zinc to prevent rusting.

Girder A large beam supporting other beams or joists.

Grain Lines in wood caused by growth.

Green Lumber Improperly seasoned lumber.

Grounds Wood strips nailed to rough walls as guides for uniform thickness of plaster.

Grout Mixture of cement, sand, and water used to seal joints and cracks.

Gutter Wood, metal, or plastic channel attached to the eaves of a house to carry off water from rain or snow.

Gypsum Board Wallboard made of gypsum with a cardboard covering.

Hanger An iron support for attaching beams; device used to fasten gutters.

Header A joist placed perpendicular to and as a support for other joists in framing for a stairway, chimney, or other opening; a lintel, or framing piece over an opening such as a door or window; a brick with its end exposed.

Hip Roof A roof that slopes upward on all sides.

Hot Spots Concentrations of lime in plaster walls that cause paint to change color.

Hydrostatic Pressure Pressure exerted by ground water against foundation walls.

Insulation Nonconducting covering on electric wire and equipment; any material placed in floors, walls, or roofs to make a house warmer in winter, cooler in summer.

Jack Post Metal support column with an adjusting screw at one end.

Jamb Side piece of a door or window opening.

Joist Timber supporting a floor or ceiling, which is in turn supported by a beam or foundation wall.

Kerf   The width of the cut made by a saw.

Keyhole Saw   Saw with a narrow, tapered blade.

Kiln-Dried   Wood seasoned in an oven, rather than in the open air.

Knee Wall   A partition that is less than full height, such as in an attic with a sloping ceiling.

Lath   Wood strips, metal, or gypsum board attached to wall studs to serve as a base for plaster.

Leader   A downspout, a pipe from a gutter to the ground.

Lintel   A horizontal structural member supporting the load over an opening such as a door or window.

Load-Bearing Wall   A wall supporting weight other than its own.

Louver   An opening with slats that allow circulation of air but exclude rain, snow, and light.

Mastic   Cement used for fastening asphalt tile and linoleum floor covering.

Miter   Joint made by fitting together two pieces cut at an angle.

Molding   Strips of wood in various designs used as trim.

Mortar   A mixture of cement and sand to bond bricks or stone.

Mortise   A hole or recessed cut, usually to receive a tenon.

Mullion   The structural division between units of windows.

Muntin   Thin strip separating panes of glass.

Muriatic Acid   Hydrochloric acid used for cleaning brickwork and concrete.

Newel   The post at the foot of a staircase.

Nipple   Short piece of pipe threaded at both ends.

Nonbearing Wall   A wall supporting no weight other than its own.

Nosing   The part of a stair thread that projects over the riser.

Oakum   Hemp or jute fiber used for caulking.

On Center From center to center, as when measuring between framing members.

Out of Plumb Not vertical or level.

Overload Drawing more electric current than a circuit or piece of equipment was designed for.

Parting Strip Strip of wood mortised into jamb of a double-hung window, separating upper and lower sash.

Partition An inside wall subdividing space within a home.

Picture Molding Molding attached to the upper part of a wall, from which pictures are hung.

Pier Masonry column, independent of the main foundation, to support other structural members.

Pigment The coloring material in paint.

Pilaster A pier that is set partly within a wall.

Pilot Hole Hole drilled as a guide for driving a screw into wood.

Pitch The slope, as for roofs or stairs, usually expressed as the ratio of the rise to the span.

Plaster Mixture of lime, cement, and sand used to cover both interior and exterior wall surfaces.

Plate Horizontal framing members atop a wall on which rest joists and rafters.

Plumb Perfectly vertical.

Plywood A board made up of three or more plies or layers of wood, glued together under pressure.

Pointing Forcing mortar into a joint after brick has been laid.

Post Timber or steel support for a beam or girder.

Pumice Stone Very finely ground stone used as a polishing abrasive.

Purlin—A horizontal framing member supporting rafters.

Putty A filler for cracks in wood or plaster; also used to fasten glass panes in window sash.

Rabbet Corner groove cut on the edge of a board, usually to form a joint.

Raceway Surface-mounted conduit for electrical wire.

292

Radius Distance from the center of a circle to the outer edge.

Rafter Structural framing member that supports a roof.

Red Lead Prime coat used when painting metal.

Reinforced Concrete Concrete strengthened by the embedment of steel bars or mesh.

Ridge The top edge where two roof surfaces meet.

Rise Vertical distance that a roof or stair rises.

Riser Vertical board between two treads in a stair. Also, pipe carrying steam or water from a boiler to radiators; a duct carrying warm air from a furnace to registers on upper floors.

Roofing The material applied to a roof to make it waterproof.

Rottenstone A fine abrasive powder used for polishing furniture.

Rubble Roughly broken stone used for construction.

Run The shortest horizontal distance from a roof ridge to the outer edge of the wall plate; the horizontal distance covered by a staircase.

Sash Frame that holds the glass in a window.

Sash Weight Metal bar suspended at end of a cord to balance sash.

Scab Short piece of lumber splicing two other pieces.

Scratch Coat The first coat of stucco or plaster.

Septic Tank A tank in which solid sewage is disintegrated by bacteria.

Sheathing Covering of boards, plywood, insulation board, or other material placed over exterior framing.

Shim A strip of wood or other material used to fill a small space.

Shingles Roofing or siding of wood or other material cut to stock sizes, sometimes in random widths.

Shiplap Boards edged to make an overlapped joint.

Shoe Molding along the bottom of baseboard, against the floor.

Sill Framing member resting on the foundation as a support for joists and other upright framing; the bottom of a window frame.

Size Glue, shellac, or varnish applied to a wall before finishing to prevent uneven absorption.

Sleeper Lumber laid on the ground or floor to support another, raised floor.

Soffit The underside of an overhang or a stair.

Soil Pipe Pipe that carries the discharge from toilets and other fixtures to the sewer system.

Soldier A brick laid on its end.

Sole Plate Horizontal framing member on which wall studs rest.

Span The distance between structural supports.

Specifications Written directions stipulating the kind, quality and sometimes the quantity of materials and workmanship required for construction.

Splash Block Concrete or other type of block laid on the ground beneath a downspout to carry drainage water away from the house.

Square A unit of measurement applied to roofing: 100 square feet.

Stile The side frame of a panel door.

Stock Size Lumber cut to standard size.

Stool The inside sill of a window frame.

Straightedge A board or other material with a straight side used for drawing and checking straight lines and flat surfaces.

Stretcher A brick laid with its greatest dimension lengthwise.

Strike Plate Metal plate on a door jamb that engages the latch bolt.

Stringer The side piece of a flight of stairs.

Stucco A rough plaster used as an exterior wall covering.

Stud Upright structural member in the framework of a house.

Subfloor Plywood or boards fastened to joists as a base for the finished floor.

Tenon A tongue cut on the end of a piece of wood to fit into a mortise on another piece.

Termite Shield Sheet metal placed on a foundation wall or around pipes to prevent the passage of termites.

Thermostat A device that responds to changes in temperature and automatically controls heating or cooling equipment.

Threshold Wood or metal beneath a door.

Throat The opening into the chimney at the top of a fireplace.

Tie Beam Structural support member that holds opposite rafters in line.

Toenailing Driving nails into wood at an angle.

Tongue-and-Groove Joint formed when the tongued edge of one board is fitted into the grooved edge of another.

Tooling Shaping the face of a mortar joint in brickwork.

Transformer A device to reduce electric voltage.

Trap Curved or looped length of pipe between a plumbing fixture and the drainage system.

Tread The horizontal part of a step.

Trim Finish molding and woodwork.

Truss A structural framework for supporting weight over long spans.

Tuck Pointing Repairing damaged joints in brickwork with fresh mortar.

Turpentine A liquid used for thinning paint.

Underlayment Material used under a finish material, such as roofing or flooring.

Union A pipe coupling that allows disconnecting of two sections of pipe without disturbing adjoining sections.

Valley The internal meeting point of two slopes of a roof.

Vehicle The liquid in a paint mixture to which pigment is added.

Veneer A thin layer of wood glued to a base of other wood.

Veneer Wall Wall with a masonry facing attached to a structural wall of another material.

Vent Stack Vertical pipe that provides circulation of air to a drainage system.

Vitrified Soil Pipe Hard-baked clay pipe used for outside sewer lines.

Volt Unit of pressure that forces amperes to flow through electric circuits.

Wainscoting Paneling or other material used to face the lower part of an interior wall.

Wallboard Gypsum board or other material in large, rigid sheets used to cover interior walls.

Water Table A projection at the bottom of an exterior wall to carry water away from the foundation.

Watt Unit of electric power, equal to amperes multiplied by volts.

Weatherstripping Narrow strips of wood, metal, rubber, felt, or other material placed around doors and windows to exclude rain, drafts, and dust.

White Lead A pigment used in paints.

Window Frame The part of a window that surrounds and holds the sash.

Index

C

298

D

Dampness:
    in basements, 20-33
    in crawl spaces, 34
    and termites and dry rot,
      34-37

Dehumidifiers,
    for basements, 32

Disc-sander, 195

Doorbells and chimes, 261-263

Doors, 138-147
    caulking of, 40-42, 51
    fitting of, 143-147
    hinges of, 139-143
    inspection of, 7, 40
    maintenance of, 281, 282
    paneled (painting of), 203
    screen repair, 156-161
    sticking, 139-143
    weatherstripping of, 163-
      168, 282

Downspouts, 95-99
    inspection of, 6, 40, 80,
      95-97
    repair of, 97-99
    and seepage, 25
    spring maintenance of, 280

Drafts, control of, 168-171
    (See also Weatherstripping)

Drainage:
    from downspouts, 99
    provisions for, 25-26
    underground, 27-29

Drain augers (snakes), 227-231

Drains (plumbing):
    clogged, 225-229
    inspection of, 8
    maintenance of, 283

Drain tiles, 27-29

Driveways, 59-78
    blacktop (See Blacktop
      driveways)
    concrete (See Concrete
      walks and driveways)
    spring maintenance of, 280

Dry rot, 34-37
    causes of, 35, 37

Dry wells (underground), 25, 27

Dusting (of basement floors),
    33

E

Efflorescence, 57

Electrical appliances:
    and blackouts, 253, 272
    cords and plugs, 253, 255-
      258, 284
    inspection of, 8
    overload of, 249-250, 253,
      272
    See also Clothes dryers

Electrical systems. See
    Circuits

Electricity, 247-263
    blackouts, 253, 271-272
    circuits (See Circuits)
    doorbells and chimes, 261-
      263
    lamp repairs, 258-261
    light switches, 253-255
    overheated wires, 269-271
    winter maintenance of, 284

P

Paint (inside):
  inspection of, 8
  mixing of, 187
  preparation for, 201
  types of, 192-193

Paint (outside):
  duration of, 57, 194-195
  fall maintenance of, 281
  inspection of, 8
  mixing of, 187
  preparation for, 195-198
  problems and cures, 198-200
  types of, 30, 194-195

Paint brushes, 182-187
  cleaning of, 184-185
  types of, 183
  use of, 183-187
  width of, 182

Painting, 4, 283
  with brushes, 182-187
  of doors (paneled), 203
  preparation for, 180-181,
    186, 195-198, 201
  with rollers, 188-190
  with spray guns, 191-192
  tools for, 181
  of windows, 202-203
  of wood siding, 44

Paint remover, 197

Paneled doors, painting of, 203

Paneling, wall, 110-111, 179

Patching:
  of brick walls, 51, 54-56
  of concrete floors, 32
  for leakage, 22-23

  of masonry walls, 51-56
  of plaster, 101-105
  of screens, 157
  of walls, 179

Pavement
  See Concrete walks and
    driveways

Peeling (outside paint problem),
  199

Periodic inspections, 5-9
  See also Maintenance
    programs

Pipes (plumbing):
  fall maintenance of, 283
  frozen, 241-244, 265-267
  insulation of, 241, 265, 283
  leaks, 236-240, 265
  sweating, 241-244

Plasterboard. See Gypsum
  wallboard

Plaster repairs, 101-105

"Plumber's friend," 226

Plumbing systems, 224-246
  cesspools, 8, 230, 245-246
  drains (See Drains)
  emergencies, 265-269
  fall maintenance of, 283
  faucets, 231-234
  pipes (See Pipes)
  septic tanks, 8, 230, 245-246
  sewer lines, 25, 230-231
  toilets, 234-236, 239

Plywood paneling, 110-111

Portland cement paint, 187

Power lines, fallen, 276-277

Pressure-reducing valves, 206

304

How to Order
Extra Copies of This Book

This book is one of a series of books which make up the complete *Instant Reference Library*. Titles currently included in the series are as follows. Other titles will be added from time to time.

Instant Spelling Dictionary
Instant English Handbook
Instant Quotation Dictionary
Instant Synonyms and Antonyms
Instant Medical Spelling Dictionary
Instant World Atlas
Instant Business Dictionary
Instant Medical Adviser
Instant Secretary's Handbook
Instant Sewing Handbook
Instant Home Repair Handbook

You may order any of the above books from your local bookstore, or send your order directly to Career Institute, Dept. 899-66, 555 East Lange Street, Mundelein, Illinois 60060. Individuals, send check or money order. No COD's. Business firms or other organizations with established credit may send purchase order and be billed after delivery. The books are available in either an attractive clothbound edition at $2.25 or a deluxe leatherette, gold-stamped edition at $2.95, less the following quantity discounts:

Quantity	Discount
1 to 5 books	None
6 to 15 books	15¢ per book
16 to 49 books	25¢ per book
50 to 149 books	35¢ per book

Orders for different titles may be combined to take advantage of the above quantity prices. On orders for three or less, add 25 cents for postage and handling. Please specify whether you wish the "Cloth" or "Deluxe" binding. Illinois residents add 5% Sales Tax.